Cradle and All

Studies in Popular Culture
M. Thomas Inge, General Editor

Cradle and All

A Cultural and Psychoanalytic Reading
of Nursery Rhymes

LUCY ROLLIN

UNIVERSITY PRESS OF MISSISSIPPI
Jackson & London

Copyright © 1992 by the University Press of Mississippi
All rights reserved
Manufactured in the United States of America

95 94 93 92   4 3 2 1

The paper in this book meets the guidelines for permanence and
durability of the Committee on Production Guidelines for Book
Longevity of the Council on Library Resources.

Library of Congress Cataloging-in-Publication Data

Rollin, Lucy.
    Cradle and all : a cultural and psychoanalytic reading of nursery
rhymes / Lucy Rollin.
        p. cm. — (Studies in popular culture)
    Includes bibliographical references and index.
    ISBN 0-87805-556-8 (alk. paper)
    1. Nursery rhymes, English—History and criticism.   2. Nursery
rhymes, American—History and criticism.   3. Children's poetry,
English—History and criticism.   4. Children's poetry, American—
History and criticism.   5. Folk poetry, American—History and
criticism.   6. Folk poetry, English—History and criticism.
7. Popular literature—History and criticism.   8. Psychoanalysis and
literature.   9. Literature and anthropology.   I. Title.
II. Series: Studies in popular culture (Jackson, Miss.)
PR976.R6   1992
398.8—dc20   91-38995
                                                                  CIP
British Library Cataloging-in-Publication data available

For

Roger

The child . . . is a hero who needs a
Homer to celebrate the terror and
beauty of mere existence. I submit
Mother Goose.

—Joan Bodger

CONTENTS

Acknowledgments   xi

Preface   xiii

CHAPTER ONE   **Jumping over the Moon** Finding the
Meaning of Nursery Rhymes   3

CHAPTER TWO   **Pussy's in the Well**
Ambivalence toward Animals   17

CHAPTER THREE   **Wooing and Wedding**
The Relationship between the Sexes   41

CHAPTER FOUR   **Baby and Me** The Complementary Uses
of Holding and Playing   75

CHAPTER FIVE   **Ten O'Clock Scholar**
Learning Culture's Lessons   103

CHAPTER SIX   **Putting Humpty Dumpty Together
Again** Rewriting Nursery Rhymes   131

Notes   145

Works Cited   151

Index   157

ACKNOWLEDGMENTS

For their belief that this project was worth pursuing: Professors Robert Detweiler, Robert Paul, Rodney Hunter, and Bradd Shore of Emory University.

For their unfailing kindness, collegiality, and encouragement: Professor M. Thomas Inge and Professor Malcolm Usrey.

For her efficiency, patience, and sensitivity as an editor: Seetha Srinivasan.

For their generous help with illustrations: Dee Jones and the staff at the de Grummond Collection in the McCain Library, Hattiesburg, Mississippi; Angeline Moscatt and the staff at the Central Children's Room, Donnell Library Center, New York Public Library; Bette Weneck and the staff in Special Collections, Milbank Memorial Library, Teachers College, Columbia University.

For laying the foundation for this and all other discussions of nursery rhymes since 1951: the work of Iona and Peter Opie.

For his advice, support, and faith, both personal and professional: Roger Rollin.

PREFACE

The practice of applying psychoanalytic principles to folktales and sayings has been well-established among analysts, literary critics, and some folklorists ever since Freud began it with his analysis of jokes. Phyllis Greenacre, Leslie Fiedler, Northrop Frye, and Alan Dundes have all offered insights into folklore based on notions of repression, dream work, unconscious symbols, id/ego/superego clashes, projection, and anxiety, to mention only a few concepts that psychoanalytic thinkers have found useful. More recently, of course, with *The Uses of Enchantment*, Bruno Bettelheim made popular the psychoanalysis of the fairy tale. Although some literary critics, folklorists, and other analysts have found fault with Bettelheim's theories, his book nonetheless reintroduced the fairy tale to popular and scholarly discussion. However, studies focusing particularly on nursery *rhymes* have appeared only sporadically, and usually in psychoanalytic journals; for example, analyst Renato J. Almansi, an editor of *American Imago*, has written on Humpty Dumpty, and Thomas Mintz has explored the history and significance of "One, two, buckle my shoe."

This book owes much to all those scholars named above, but it differs from their approach in one major way. Instead of treating only one rhyme or a small handful of rhymes, it focuses on a large body of rhymes—a fragmentary and disorderly group at best.

In an attempt to find some parameters, I chose as my chief source *The Oxford Dictionary of Nursery Rhymes*, edited by Iona and Peter Opie, first published in 1951 and still the most comprehensive and enlightened collection of these rhymes available. It contains 550 rhymes, each in its fullest known version, placed in a roughly alphabetical order by the most prominent word in the first line, and then numbered. (Rhymes taken from the Opie collection that appear in this book are followed by the number the Opies assigned them; numbers *not* preceded by *No.* are, of course, page numbers.) I supplemented the Opie rhymes with a few from William and Ceil Baring-Gould's collection, *The Annotated Mother Goose*, which appeared in 1962 and contains almost twice as many rhymes as the Opies'. Though the Baring-Goulds' book is overall less scholarly than the Opies', it does call attention to the American contribution to the rhymes and to the intricate relationship between the American and English versions—a point of view I found interesting and occasionally helpful. (Rhymes in my book that were borrowed from this collection are identified with "B-G" and the number the Baring-Goulds assigned them.)

After limiting myself to these sources for the rhymes, I explored ways of grouping them, and decided that they fell naturally, for my purpose, into the categories animal rhymes, courtship and marriage rhymes, lullabies and amusements, and didactic rhymes. These categories provide the arrangement and focus of the chapters. I then looked for psychological and cultural patterns within those loose groupings. I found a good deal of cruelty toward animals, which was balanced overall with tenderness, and the coexistence of these attitudes suggested ambivalence toward other species. The large number of courtship and marriage rhymes revealed not romance but a prickly relationship between the sexes, possibly grounded in the fear of women—something English-speaking culture shares with many others—as well as the combination of the strongly individualistic and mercantile attitudes toward courting and marrying that seems to distinguish English culture. The lullabies and amusements, those rhymes that accompany various touching and holding activities between adult and child, showed an interesting balance between gentleness—both in action and language—and rougher treatment such as hitting, pinching, and jouncing; both modes of touching seem to be important in the culture. ABC and counting rhymes naturally have teaching as their purpose, but I found that tongue twisters and riddles, which constitute some of the best-known rhymes, also encourage learning, though of less obvious lessons.

As I began to discuss my work with colleagues and acquaintances, I found them often asking what I was going to say about "Cinderella" or about "Hansel and Gretel." I realized that a great many people think of the nursery rhymes and fairy tales as one entity and that I would need to clarify the difference between them. I have done this in my opening pages. I also found that people were generally aware of some of the discomfort the rhymes have caused and of efforts to revise them—to say of the Old Woman in the Shoe, for example, "She *kissed* them all soundly" instead of "She *whipped* them all soundly." These efforts have a lengthy but scattered history, and raise many interesting questions about shifting values within the culture. I have offered some analysis of this complex issue in my closing chapter.

My chief reason for choosing a psychoanalytic approach to these rhymes is personal preference. I find psychoanalytic theory a congenial and informative way of looking at human behavior and at literature. But there are more defensible reasons. One is, of course, that psychoanalysis gives preference to one's earliest years, and these rhymes are firmly associated with childhood—although, as the Opies demonstrate, their origins may be adult. More importantly, psychoanalysis directly acknowledges the importance of the body, as it observes the tension between our sexuality and our social role and the working out of this tension through language. In Elizabeth Wright's phrase, psychoanalysis helps us understand "bodies speaking to bodies, not merely minds speaking to minds" (5)—a particularly apt way to describe the relationship between a mother and a young child who are sharing "This little pig."

Like other recent psychoanalytic critics, my overall approach tends away from classical Freudian concerns such as the death drive or the Oedipus complex, and toward object relations and ego psychology. To me, the nursery rhymes suggest the containment of strong urges and the use of defensive and adaptive maneuvers in the service of maturation. Object relations theory, with its focus on the powerful fantasies of early childhood, the importance of the fantasy-mother, and the defenses of projection and introjection, provides a helpful focus on the strong feelings that emerge from the rhymes. Ego psychology, with its emphasis on conscious and unconscious defenses and its recognition of the importance of the environment, offers a vocabulary for seeing the rhymes in a cultural context, especially didactic rhymes such as counting and ABC rhymes.

A recent issue of the annual *Children's Literature* (Vol. 18, 1990) offered cogent commentary on the pitfalls of psychoanalytic literary criticism and the necessity for caution in its application. U. C. Knoepflmacher calls for multiple perspectives, Patrick Horgan for a more scientific method, and Jack Zipes for the inclusion of historical and social evidence in psychoanalytic interpretations (125–43). Although I cannot claim a broad enough approach to satisfy all of these desiderata, I have attempted to supplement my psychoanalytic interpretations with other kinds of material, most notably from cultural anthropology and history. Like psychoanalysis, these too are interpretive disciplines. Both suggest that the events and products of human culture are not nonsensical or illogical but have links to the material culture on the one hand, and on the other to the individuals who inhabit that culture. And although such interpretations involve, to borrow Clifford Geertz's words, "guessing at meanings, assessing the guesses, and drawing explanatory conclusions from the better guesses" (20), the "guessing" that constitutes history, psychoanalysis, ethnography, and literary criticism often yields useful insights about what it means to be human in a particular time, in a particular place.

For example, one of the most interesting results of my research has been the discovery that psychoanalytic interpretations of literature, and especially of folk literature, are often validated from the "inside," as it were: from the clinical practice of psychoanalysts. Analysands sometimes refer to themselves as a fairy tale or nursery rhyme character in their efforts to describe and understand their situations. Analysts in turn may use this material to interpret further the analysand's problems or to shed light on a general phenomenon, such as using the term "Humpty Dumpty" to describe neurotic symptoms based on the theme of bodily fragility. Such associations would not occur without the shared language of nursery rhymes.

Thus, although my approach here is generally that of psychoanalytic literary interpretation, I have tried to supplement it with history, with cultural anthropology, and with occasional clinical material. I hope this eclectic approach will make the book informative and interesting even to those readers not persuaded by the validity of psychoanalysis. Let me also add that nowhere do I mean to suggest any prescriptive use of the rhymes with children. I believe that, in general, children tend to find and use whatever cultural elements they need to help them deal with their particular and current psychological situations. Making the rhymes generally available might be helpful—like keeping fruit in the kitchen and hoping the child will choose it over cookies—but I believe children are not generally persuaded when an adult shares a book or a nursery rhyme because it might be "good for them." Much more powerful—and more fun, in the long run—is the spontaneous sharing of a rhyme the adult enjoyed in childhood and remembers naturally, when a moment of genuine closeness brings it to mind.

Finally, a word about my own position on the many efforts to revise the rhymes—to write new but familiar-sounding rhymes on current subjects such as ecology, or, as much more frequently happens, to remove the violence and sexism from them. I prefer to accept the violence in the rhymes as a psychologically healthful element, allowing children and adults to express hostile thoughts in a relatively harmless manner, as do most of us who watch Clint Eastwood movies, read crime fiction, or enjoy football.

I have more difficulty accepting the sexism in them, especially when it is coupled with violence. There is no doubt that the rhymes have done their part, as have most other forms of popular and folk entertainment, to perpetuate the subjugation of women in our society. Nonetheless, I suggest the rhymes remain unbowdlerized. Removing sexist elements from the rhymes might, over time, have a salutary effect, but only if such changes were accompanied by broader changes in other forms of popular and folk culture and in our laws. Meanwhile, for myself, I accept the rhymes as they are, acknowledging their warts and hoping that what we learn from them is much more than the sum of those particular parts.

Cradle and All

Figure 1. Jack and Jill. Anonymous illustration from *Little Boy Blue: A Collection of Nursery Rhymes*. de Grummond Children's Literature Research Collection.

Hey diddle diddle,
The cat and the fiddle,
The cow jumped over the moon;
The little dog laughed
To see such sport,
And the dish ran away with the spoon.

CHAPTER 1 **Jumping over the Moon**
Finding the Meaning
of Nursery Rhymes

Such casual, cheerful nonsense has delighted children for centuries, engaging their tongues and teasing their imaginations. Adults too have enjoyed such nonsense rhymes, but, being adults and uncomfortable with what they cannot explain, have relegated them to the nursery—where they refuse to stay. For many years, both amateur and professional scholars have tried to discover the meaning of nursery rhymes, recording their attempts in books, journals, and even films. Though some of these efforts may seem as curious as a cow jumping over the moon, they are always fascinating and have often found their way into popular lore.

The first problem any nursery-rhyme scholar must address is what to call these rhymes. The British usually call them "nursery rhymes," and Americans say "Mother Goose rhymes." However, "Mother Goose" originally referred to what we now call fairy tales, such as "Cinderella" and "Puss in Boots"; the name first appeared in print in 1697, when Charles Perrault published *Contes de my mere l'oye*—"Tales of my mother goose." Perhaps this is one reason some people still think of nursery rhymes and fairy tales as a single entity. In this book, to keep the distinction clear, I have chosen to call them nursery rhymes.

On the other hand, there are several good reasons for equating the tales and the rhymes. Both are folk literature, the products of anonymous authors, which have lasted for centuries and have been disseminated largely by oral transmission. Both fairy tales and nursery rhymes exist in many cultures and share many symbols and motifs. Both were generally intended for adult audiences but have become associated with the "nursery"—where children are assumed to enjoy amusements quite different from those of adults. Both have, as a result of this isolation in the nursery, become a part of "children's literature," an amorphous genre curiously separate from literature for adults in most people's minds. Both offer elements of straightforward fantasy: animals talk, objects dance, a full-grown adult may be the size of a thumb or, conversely, large enough to ingest other human beings in one gulp.

The tales and rhymes also share certain literary features. Just as the tales often contain small poems or rhythmic and repetitive elements, which resemble nursery rhymes, the rhymes often tell stories. "Jack and Jill" is a fascinating little narrative with a distinct beginning, middle, and end packed into a tiny space. "A frog he would a-wooing go" has the rollicking elements of a Fielding novel. "There was a little man, And he wooed a little maid" is a generic saga of courtship.

However, there are some distinct and important differences between the tales and the rhymes.[1] The characters that inhabit fairy tales are often extraordinary in some way—the most beautiful, the smallest, the fiercest. Their exotic names reflect not only their extraordinariness—Beauty, Bluebeard—but sometimes their European origins as well, as with Rapunzel (German for the vegetable rampion). The characters in the rhymes are generally much more ordinary, as are their resolutely English names: Jack, Sue, Mrs. Bond, Elsie, Simon. They carry on their activities in the barnyard, kitchen, tavern, or village street, as opposed to the mysterious forests, exotic castles, and strange lakes and rivers that surround the fairy-tale characters. And although the tales tend to focus on the young, often with the old as adversary, the rhymes depict all ages, from infancy to callow youth to middle age to dotage. In the tales, appearance is often an indicator of morality; the beautiful tend to be good, the ugly wicked. No such code exists for the rhymes.

The rhymes and tales share motifs, but express them differently. Both often describe journeys, but in the tales, these journeys are often long, even years long, and to exotic places by some exotic means—magic boots, a magic wishing ring. In the rhymes, the journey is likely to involve only a trip into town on a wagon, and then "home again, home again, jiggety jig." Journeys in the tales may not have a clear purpose—to "seek one's fortune," for instance. In the rhymes, the characters usually have a practical purpose: to fetch a pail of water, to buy ribbons at a fair, to sell a pig. Gifts are a common motif in the rhymes and the tales. But whereas the tales tend to offer magic keys or jewels or lamps, the rhymes offer strawberries and cream, a paper of pins, or a simple, unmagical wedding ring. Love and marriage figure prominently in both the rhymes and the tales, but in the tales, love is often at first sight and highly romantic, with marriage taking place offstage, after the "happily ever after." In the rhymes, courtship is often irritating (one maid turns her suitor into the hog tub), and marriage is at its worst quarrelsome and violent, and at its best a resigned compromise.

One can find exceptions to all these generalizations in both the tales and rhymes, but on the whole the worlds depicted in them differ significantly. Folklorist Sheila Ingersoll examined a body of the rhymes in comparison with the tales and noted that 75 percent of the tales ended happily, whereas 84 percent of the rhymes ended "unhappily," an assessment that could apply to a variety of situations. Assigning numbers and percentages to such judgments is risky, but it does reveal, in Ingersoll's phrase, that the world of tales is "far simpler and neater" than that of the rhymes (45). The tales seem optimistic—or artificially unrealistic—about the future, compared to the general pessimism—or realism—about marriage, money, and children that infuses the rhymes and implies that maturation is a series of difficult compromises with oneself and others.

Ingersoll further notes that the tales speak in the past tense while the rhymes often speak in the present, or occasionally in and of the future, suggesting differences in points of view. The tales, it seems, offer a way to restructure or think about the past; the rhymes, in contrast, describe what *is* and on occasion what we hope for. Thus the rhymes and tales are "complementary responses to the human condition" (Ingersoll, 52), both necessary modes of understanding ourselves.

Despite all these differences, the shared association with childhood and the nursery probably accounts for the fact that most people think of the rhymes and the tales as a single entity. But nursery rhymes also share important elements with something generally associated more with adulthood: jokes. Both jokes and rhymes are short, both are little vignettes of life, and like jokes, nursery rhymes often end in a "punch line." Old Mother Hubbard's effort to communicate with her dog seems to be going well as the dog bows to her, but then he can only say, in the last line of the rhyme, "Bow wow!" In "If all the seas were one sea," the images become larger and larger, more and more impressive, until they culminate in, not the great sounding crash we are led to expect, but only a "splish-splash." Any adult who has enjoyed rhymes with a child knows that part of their pleasure is the shared laugh that almost invariably follows their recitation.

Freud called jokes "developed play," and said that they were the "most social of all the mental functions that aim at a yield of pleasure" (1905, 179). He described what he called the "joke work," and, in one of his characteristic leaps of insight, compared it to the work of dreams: the use of condensation, abbreviation, substitute formation, and displacement of emphasis, all in the service of disguising taboo thoughts under a funny or nonsensical surface. This is not difficult to see in hostile or obscene jokes, which get their pleasurable effects from rebellion against authority, from saying or imagining something ordinarily prohibited in polite society. Freud often cited the number of cynical jokes about marriage, pointing out that such jests provide a way of saying that marriage really does not satisfy the needs it pretends to (1905, 111–12). Many nursery rhymes do precisely the same thing, such as "Tom married a wife on Sunday," ostensibly an amusing rhyme to teach the days of the week but one which describes Tom beating and eventually killing his wife; its punch line is "Glad was Tom on Saturday night, To bury his wife on Sunday."

But there are more subtle forms of joke work that the rhymes share: plasticity of language and symbol, allusions, double meanings, and absurdity are all useful for expressing ordinarily hidden thoughts. For example, "Henry was a worthy king" begins with what seems a straightforward description of gifts between Henry and Mary, but shifts the focus in the closing stanza:

Henry was a worthy king,
Mary was his queen,
He gave to her a lily,
Upon a stalk of green.

Then for all his kindness,
And for all his care,
She gave him a new-laid egg
In the garden there.

Love, can you sing?
  I cannot sing.
A story tell?
  Not one I know.
Then let us play at king and queen
As down the garden walks we go. (B-G, no. 193)

A lily and an egg seem rather commonplace gifts for a "worthy king" and his queen, despite their beauty and natural value. Perhaps they symbolize a wedding and sexual consummation, with symbols of male (lily on a stalk) and female (egg) substituting for a ring and ritual as well for intercourse. The shift in the third stanza, signaled by "Love," seems at first abrupt and nonsensical. But it changes the impersonal comment of the first two stanzas' description of royal lovers to an intimate exchange of words between more mundane lovers, and "playing at king and queen" becomes sexual play, which may be more entertaining, or simply more possible, than singing or storytelling. And even impoverished or untalented lovers can become "royalty" if they marry and have children, at least in the imaginations of those children. The rhyme therefore becomes a form of graceful seduction. Of course, one could find much more in this simple rhyme, and that is precisely the point: the rhymes use processes similar to dreams and jokes—substitution, symbols, condensation, abbreviation—to create multiple levels of meaning.

Most people know approximately what the "id" means in classical psychoanalysis: the part of the psyche that harbors our drives and our forbidden (by society and by ourselves) thoughts and wishes. Less commonly understood is the process by which those drives and wishes push their way to the surface (as they always try to do; hence the need for defenses, both conscious and unconscious). Freud called it the primary process (1965 [1901] 626–48). In his view, its chief aim is the discharge of tension and energy resulting from unsatisfied drives, which it achieves by several means. It condenses its attention from several elements onto a single element, thus investing that element with disproportionate interest and energy. It forms compromises and constructs intermediate ideas, operating with little selectivity about such elements and their importance. It creates very loose links among ideas, often treating mere verbal similarities as equal to substantive likeness. Finally, in primary-process thinking, contradictory ideas stand side by side as if there were no contradiction.

Such processes are usually rejected by the conscious mind as illogical and nonsensical. However, they surface quite often in jokes, dreams, folklore of various sorts—including and especially nursery rhymes—and all kinds of high and popular art, because in these genres the primary process acquires some logical form. It is subjected to what Freud terms the secondary process: the imposition of some accepted form, in which the links are clear, the contradictions resolved, and the energy diffused. We all engage in the secondary process when we tell a dream: though the dream itself was strange and illogical, and perhaps unsettling, when we tell it to someone, we change it into a narrative, possibly one with a punch line—"And then she turned into my *mother!*" In the rhyme quoted earlier about King Henry, sexual coupling acquires poetic form and order in a pleasant metaphor about a garden, a lily, an egg, and a companionable walk.

The rhymes are full of primary-process thinking, with their loose links among ideas, verbal play, and use of aural similarities to stand for more logical ones. Jack uses his *thumb* to get a *plum;* little kittens wash their mittens; a *cow* jumps over the *moo*n. They are also full of infantile notions such as feats of devouring, cutting off body parts, beating, and soiling. Child psychiatrist Vincent de Santis finds that very popular rhymes such as "Rub a dub dub," "Mistress Mary," "Little Bo-Peep," and "There was a crooked man" represent what he calls the "prototype of the nursery rhyme genre," because they "rely so much on primary process, the child's archaic mode of experience." For this reason, he says, our responses to them "are more unconscious and personal" (620). But since all of it comes under the sway of the secondary process, the effect is usually pleasurable or even funny. Freud commented that this is the usual result when the primary process becomes conscious: its energy is discharged in laughter (1968 [1901], 644).[2]

Of course, what distinguishes rhymes from jokes, finally, is that they are *poetry*. They operate symbolically, like poetry, as we have seen, but more basically, their most characteristic feature is their rhythmic patterns and their rhymes. In any given collection of rhymes, one can find almost every known poetic form, with one exception: free verse. Nursery rhymes always rhyme and always have an easily discernible rhythm. They are not "free," but are tightly controlled forms, with their multilayered messages packed into very small spaces.

The power of this condensation of language becomes particularly noticeable in L. Frank Baum's efforts to revise the rhymes. In 1899, the man who would become famous as the author of *The Wonderful Wizard of Oz* (1900) turned a number of nursery rhymes into prose tales: *Mother Goose in Prose*. Baum was certainly a natural storyteller, and the rhymes offered him an opportunity to expand on their characters and situations. Baum thus gives the "reason" for several of the rhymes, explaining that Little Boy Blue fell asleep under the haystack because he had been up all night caring for his injured mother, that Old King Cole was merry because he was a commoner accidentally chosen as monarch, and that Mistress Mary Quite Contrary planted her garden to help her pass the time until her traveling father returned. Though the little tales are imaginative, they strain to make all the details in the rhymes fit into some sort of prose context. And instead of the lively and somewhat mysterious rebels they are in the rhymes, the characters become conventional good children, their odd behavior explained away. But most importantly, these prose retellings lack the power and vitality of the originals because they lack the rhythm and rhyme of the originals. "Translating" them into prose has taken from them their almost ritualistic power to charm.

Analyst Thomas Mintz has suggested that the source of this power in the rhymes is their association with feeding. He believes that rhythmic sucking at the breast may be the "most important experiential event in life of an infant" (24, no. 2), and he argues that there is a likely connection between feeding and more abstract acculturation in infancy. At the same time that a child rhythmically ingests food, it presumably absorbs the love and attention of the parent, the pattern of holding that the culture has bequeathed to the parent, and the culture's language patterns as well, as the parent talks or sings to the child or responds to its sounds.

The connections between culture and child care have occasionally seemed to confound those who study cultural patterns. Geoffrey Gorer's work is the most controversial on this point. Part of the post-World War II effort to study the collective psyches of nations such as Russia and Japan, an effort in which Margaret Mead and Ruth Benedict also participated, Gorer developed his "swaddling hypothesis"—the notion that the Russian practice of swaddling infants produced the Russian social and political character (long periods of inactivity alternating with bursts of intense social interaction). Although Gorer did not claim a causal relationship but found identities between culture and personality (Bock 85), many scholars have felt he was indeed claiming that one caused the other, and his reputation as a cultural anthropologist has suffered. His 1955 study of English character, however, although some of its conclusions may be suspect, allowed the many anonymous respondents to his questionnaires to reveal to a surprising degree the conflict between different kinds of behaviors that inhabit any individual member of a culture. The responses to Gorer's questionnaires, sounding oftentimes like an analysand's free associations, show the same configuration of attitudes toward animals, child rearing, and the relationship between the sexes as do the rhymes. As a result, they have constituted for me a kind of clinical data, which I could not have obtained elsewhere and which, I believe, lend credence to some of my conclusions about the rhymes, their bodily origins, and the cultural patterns embedded in them and hence disseminated by them. (Gorer's material will appear at various times later in this book.)

Géza Róheim, a trained analyst who conducted ethnographic fieldwork among the Marquesans and the Navajo, stressed the prolonged infancy of the human being and the implications of that infancy for cultural conditioning. He saw the existence of symbolism and of certain human traits as due to this "universal neoteny of mankind" (491), and sounds Jungian in his belief that "there can be many types of culture but only one unconscious" (491). Some of the rhymes' motifs resemble those in the myths of other cultures, such as the fantasy of the phallic woman, and the image of the fragile egg/human in "Humpty Dumpty." Probably the prolonged infancy of our species and its physical implications of fragility and dependency have helped to produce the rich residues of folklore that have found their way into the nursery rhymes.

But the idea that has come closest to expressing the connection between culture and the individual is that of projection. Cultural anthropologists have borrowed this concept from psychology and applied it to their work; the resultant insights have helped to express the intricate link between the individual and culture.

Classical Freudian psychoanalysis tends to emphasize repression as the most fundamental human psychological defense, and indeed the concept of repression is among the most basic of all psychoanalytic concepts. Briefly, it is a normal and pervasive defense in which forbidden thoughts or wishes are *unconsciously* pushed into oblivion so completely that we forget we ever had them. Few human beings could function in their daily lives without engaging in repression. The complementary defensive process, one equally common and normal—and equally unconscious—is projection. In it, the offending idea or wish is not forgotten; on the contrary, it is acknowledged but as the property of someone or something else, and we disclaim responsibility for it.

Melanie Klein and her adherents in the English school of psychoanalysis believe that projection may be one of the earliest mental activities of the infant, that the child at its mother's breast projects its aggressive impulses outward even onto the mother herself. Whether or not one chooses to accept this notion (and most theorists acknowledge that any chronological arrangement of defenses is only speculative), we can see projection operating in very young children when they attribute hostility or cruelty to an animal, a piece of furniture, or another child or adult, when it is obviously they who feel hostile. Of course, perfectly normal adults also engage in a form of it when they attribute, for example, their lack of employment success solely to the federal government or to a boss who doesn't like them.[3]

It is the contention of several thinkers that projection happens on a larger scale as well, and that the products of a collective human effort, such as nursery rhymes, are the result of a culture's projection of the inner concerns of its people.

Abram Kardiner, a trained analyst, worked with anthropologist Ralph Linton to develop the notion of primary and secondary institutions within a given society. Primary institutions are those governing the subsistence of a culture, such as its food-gathering practices, or governing its child-rearing practices, such as weaning or toileting. Secondary institutions are such elements as folklore and religion, which result from the unconscious attribution of one's own wishes and fears to someone or something external; they are "projective systems," and constitute the "matrix out of which the character formation of the individual takes place up to late childhood," and in turn reinforce those institutions or practices from which they arise (Kardiner, 361, 235). Kardiner believed that such secondary institutions could not be studied in themselves, but only through their interaction with the personalities of those who inhabit the culture (25).

Kardiner's theory of institutions is analogous in part to Freud's theory of primary and secondary process. The primary institutions, like the primary process, are governed by basic bodily needs; the secondary institutions, like the secondary process, operate defensively to order and control the desires associated with those needs, and are highly adaptable to individuals. Among English-speaking cultures, for example, child-rearing practices involve certain kinds of holding; the child is normally held closely and gently while being fed or put to sleep, but when the child is being played with, the handling becomes rougher, as the parent bounces or pretends to drop the child. The nursery rhymes, as a secondary institution growing out of such practices, give form to such activities in lullabies and in various kinds of knee-dandling, bouncing games, which in turn reinforce the idea that such activities are pleasurable and worthy of being passed on to the next generation. Kardiner's theory helps to explain the persistence of such practices over long periods of time, since it suggests a connection, within each individual, between a culture's solutions to the basic challenges of existence and its shared folklore and rituals.

Alan Dundes, a psychoanalytic folklorist, also perceives folklore as a projective system. It operates defensively to provide a "socially sanctioned outlet for the expression of what cannot be articulated in the more usual, direct way" (1980, 36). It unconsciously ascribes to the outside world painful, unacceptable, or taboo feelings and impulses experienced by the individual, expressing those feelings in jokes, sayings, tales, songs, and nursery rhymes embedded in the culture. He calls folklore "autobiographical ethnography . . . a mirror of culture" (38), although deciphering its meaning is not easy, for projections are unconscious and not quickly accessible to analysis.

Projection shares with dreams one technique that occasionally sheds light on its meaning: the literalization of metaphor. A friend once, at a time of uncertainty about advising his grown child, dreamed of walking with that same child as a five-year-old through the side streets of a city, unable to find the main road because he lacked a map. Such a dream literally expressed the metaphoric connection between child raising and an uncertain journey. Dundes cites the old woman in the shoe as a literalization of the metaphor of the shoe as a symbol of marriage and childbearing or as a symbol of the female genitalia (1980, 45–47; 1987, 31–32). In the rhymes, pet keeping is a common metaphor for marriage—from the male point of view; as the rhymes literalize it, wives become hens, cats, or cows. Such literalization is a form of projection and defense against the repressed wish for, say, a wife as mute and placid as a cow. In such rhymes, Dundes believes, folklore has provided members of English-speaking cultures with a way to express a taboo wish by unconsciously believing that someone else—whoever anonymously composed the rhyme—wished it. These rhymes are one way we deal with what Dundes aptly calls "cultural pressure points," such as the need to marry and bear children, and with individual anxieties, such as those about sex (1980, x). Many people are uncomfortable with the assigning of such meanings to nursery rhymes. They feel that sexual allusions surely could not be present in material meant for children. But one anonymous illustrator from the late nineteenth century evidently sensed—as have more recent theorists—that Jack and Jill's fall down the hill was a literalized metaphor for sex; he or she drew a kissing couple spilling water, instead of two little children (Figure 1).

Of course, many of the best-known rhymes were the product of the seventeenth century (Opie, 6–7), a time when adults were less particular about what children ate, drank, saw, or heard, and that might partially account for their frequent surface or hidden bawdiness. That the lusty characters and vignettes in these rhymes have continued to fascinate us up to the present, however, suggests that something more elemental is at work. As the product of adult minds aimed at children, these rhymes intend to communicate something, consciously or unconsciously, about life in English-speaking cultures.

Just what that something is, however, has been the subject of a number of scholarly efforts, and much disagreement. The most remarkable example of such scholarship is that of John Bellenden Ker, whose treatise, *An Essay on the Archaeology of Popular English Phrases and Nursery Rhymes*, first appeared in 1834. In this strange document, Ker argued that the rhymes were originally written in an early form of Dutch (actually a language of his own invention) and that, when translated back into English, the rhymes took on considerable political significance. "Little Bo-Peep," for instance, became "Littel boo-piep hys lost is suijpe," which meant "Our little Boo-peep is too fond of his cup," which in turn meant, "The friar who begged support for the monastery—he intruded into every home for provisions and idle gossip" (132). Indeed, Ker believed the rhymes "translated" as a body into an expression of "the intrusion of a foreign and onerous church-sway, bringing with it a ministry, to which a goaded people imputed fraud and exaction" (Ker, 122). The Opies call Ker's efforts "probably the most extraordinary example of misdirected labor in the history of English letters" (27–28), but it must have had its charms for it was revised and republished at least three times during Ker's life.

A more recent and more widely disseminated example of this search for meaning in Mother Goose comes from the United States. Katherine Elwes Thomas's *The Real Personages of Mother Goose* has been surprisingly influential since its first appearance in Boston in 1930. Many people seem to have been attracted to its mixture of fact and fiction and to have found comfort in Thomas's assertions that the characters in Mother Goose rhymes are historical personages. She insists, for example, that "Humpty Dumpty" refers to Richard III fallen to Bosworth (39), that Jack and Jill are Cardinal Wolsey and Bishop Tarbes (91), that the runaway dish and spoon are "undoubtedly Edward Earl of Hertford . . . and the Lady Katharine Grey" (141), that Bo-Peep is Mary Queen of Scots, that Curly Locks is Charles II, and so on. Thomas did plenty of research in various libraries in England, and traveled the countryside, evidently absorbing fact and folklore indiscriminately, in her search for the meaning of Mother Goose. Her book has been made into an MGM documentary, which, according to Perry Nodelman, "probably put these silly theories into popular circulation where . . . they still survive" (188).

Albert Mason Stevens, a Rhodes scholar at Oxford from 1905 to 1908, formed a club with Max Beerbohm, Julian Huxley, and others to do "research" on unlikely topics. Stevens chose nursery rhymes. His efforts were not published until 1968, but they make amusing reading: he depends less on anecdote and trivia than Thomas, but is almost as imaginative as Ker, especially in his excursions into etymology. For instance, he arrives at a theory identifying Jack and Jill's pail of water as the "pael of Walter"—that is, a "sacred vestment" of Archbishop Hubert Walter, and he has some ingenious evidence for the speculation (121–28).

Historians Robert Darnton and William J. Baker have emphasized the value of the rhymes as a corrective to seeing history too much in terms of politics and war. Darnton believes we need to reread Mother Goose in order to imagine "lives that really were nasty, brutish, and short" (29); Baker believes the rhymes tell us "how vastly different the past was from the present" (651–52). The meaning of the rhymes, for these historians, is as a record of material culture— certainly not a bad use for them, but one that begs the question: if life really was so very different, why do we still enjoy these rhymes and share so many of them with our children? There must be some other relevance to "Humpty Dumpty" and "Little Bo-Peep" if children still know and love them today.

Katherine Elwes Thomas gave an interesting clue to this relevance in her opening pages, as she describes the origin of her research:

> It had its inception in a never-to-be-forgotten incident of my childhood, when, standing beside my mother as she sang, "Ride a cock horse to Banbury Cross," she smilingly remarked, "The old woman on the white horse was Queen Elizabeth." This comment, made with the certainty of one who repeats a well-known fact, convinced me that somewhere in England and the Colonies there must have existed a traditionary knowledge of the original import of all these delightful rhymes. (16)

Upon such a small moment, "inescapably lodged in that far, faint memory," Thomas spent twenty-five years of elucidation. Would she have done so if the remark had had a more distant source? The power of the remark, though it seems to lie in the suggestion of a historical puzzle, is rooted in a more elemental context: the close physical and verbal interaction between mother and child. This is the context that impelled Thomas to seek answers, and it is the context in which the nursery rhymes are most often communicated.

The strange characters, bizarre situations, rhythm and rhyme, and the accompanying physical activity that we associate with the rhymes are first experienced, for most of us, within that parent-child context. Moreover, we first heard them when language was for us still a great mystery, something fraught with meaning and enormous significance, which we could not grasp. To the infant, language is a riddle that must be solved; otherwise all is chaos. Our discomfort with apparent meaninglessness may result from that early perception and cause us to seek meaning wherever we can find it in these apparently nonsensical rhymes, just as we did as infants in the sounds adults made. And "in revealing the power of language to make the ordinary wonderful and to be wonderful in and for itself," the rhymes remind us of that early wonder and of our initiation into the mysteries of language (Nodelman, 198).

Mother Goose, then, is far from meaningless, although the meanings may not be the ones scholars like Thomas and Stevens have sought. Instead of historical events, the rhymes communicate the most elementary of concerns of the culture to its children—concerns about nature, food, sex, and language. They also express, in their bodily rhythms and symbols, the most elementary concerns of the child. In Vincent de Santis's words, the rhymes "are the first cultural experience with language used as a tool to convey a sense of the inner experience of one's body, feelings about oneself, desires for attachment, worry about separation, and the fears and hopes concerning aggressive and sexual urges" (604). By symbolically acknowledging these concerns, the rhymes offer an opportunity for adults to say to children, even unconsciously, "Yes, we know how it is; we remember"—and to offer at the same time the means of control through social interaction, and through language.

Ding, dong, bell,
Pussy's in the well.
Who put her in?
Little Johnny Green.
Who pulled her out?
Little Johnny Stout.
What a naughty boy was that.
To try to drown poor pussy cat,
Who never did him any harm,
And killed the mice in his father's barn.

CHAPTER 2 **Pussy's in the Well**
Ambivalence toward
Animals

The nursery rhymes describing animals seem at first to range over a considerable variety of species and to encompass a number of different attitudes toward them. But upon closer examination, distinct patterns emerge. One is the focus on the domestic animal. Writers of literary nonsense such as Edward Lear and Lewis Carroll may invent fantastic creatures for our enjoyment, but the anonymous authors of the rhymes have contented themselves with horses, dogs, birds, cats, hens, cows, and pigs. Of course, this focus may result partly from the English rural way of life; the rhymes simply deal with the animals the English know best. But a life so closely intertwined with these animals produces interesting emotional configurations and contrasts: gratitude toward them and their life-sustaining products yet disgust at their habits, appreciation for their faithfulness yet ridicule for their stupidity. The rhymes seems to reflect this ambivalence, as they balance cruelty and kindness and acknowledge

Figure 2. Ding dong bell. Anonymous illustration from *The Only True Mother Good Melodies.* The Central Children's Room, Donnell Library Center, The New York Public Library.

the need for self-control in the company of the animals we have tamed and on which we depend.

The Juvenile Cabinet of Natural History, published in London in 1806, offers a classification of animals most connected with English life. The horse, described and illustrated first in the book, is "noble and useful," blessed with courage, spirit, ardor, patience, and perseverance. The cow "adds less to man's splendour than the horse" but cares for man's daily needs with every "atom" of its useful body. The sheep is also useful, the female of the species especially loving to her offspring. The dog's most notable characteristics are his willingness to save humans and his faithfulness—to humans, of course. The hog, the last animal in the book, is "filthy," with a "dull, drowsy look." The hog is "useless during life, and like the miser, [provides] benefit only by his death."

Such a taxonomy, with its surface ranking by usefulness, its conviction of superiority, and its underlying anthropomorphism, reveals the popular thinking about animals in England during the sixteenth through the eighteenth centuries, the period when most of the English nursery rhymes were composed and recorded (Opie, 6–7). Prior to this time, the ascendant philosophy identified all nature as designed for man's use; Adam's domination of Eden was theological proof that human beings were meant to dominate the natural world, and the human and animal estates were completely separate. As the known world expanded, however, and nature came to include more unclassifiable and possibly unconquerable species, the notion of absolute husbandry underwent a shift. Gradually, animals became less a divine trust and more a separate estate onto which human beings could project their thoughts about themselves. This change is particularly noticeable in English culture; during this time England moved from being known as the nation most cruel to animals, to that practicing the most tender sensibilities toward them. Bearbaiting as a sport gave way to the Royal Society for the Prevention of Cruelty to Animals, and by 1869 even fox hunting faced charges of cruelty to the fox (Thomas, 164). The English have always been dependent on animals for their survival, but this shift in attitude marks a transition to a greater awareness of that dependency and consequently, from a psychoanalytic standpoint, to a greater ambivalence about the animals on which they depend—not unlike a child's ambivalence toward its parents, or an employee's toward the owner of the business. These attitudes contain a mixture of affection, admiration, irritation, fear, and hate, which reveals itself in various projections. Such projections, in turn, work themselves out in rhymes that, in Dundes's words, "provide an unconscious screen or arena for the display of the causes of anxiety, and it is for this reason that folkloristic projections are so indispensable as tools in the human arsenal for mental health" (Dundes 1980, 45).

The sadistic component in the human personality has always been a puzzle. Freud allied it with sexual development as an integral part of the pregenital period, specifically the anal stage, when aggressive instincts are strong and the drive toward mastery dominates development. Such instincts often find their objects in animals, and although these drives may be tamed in adulthood, they do not disappear. By 1923, after considerable thought, Freud believed that sadism was the representative of the "second class of instincts"—that is, the death instinct, acting in opposition to Eros to bring the organism into a state of quiescence: life itself is "a conflict and compromise between these two trends" (1960 [1923], 30–31). By 1930, in *Civilization and Its Discontents*, Freud clung even more tenaciously to his notion of a death instinct; when it merges with Eros, it becomes sadism—that is, endowed with pleasurable feelings. In this compromised form, it exists not only in spite of, but as a representative of, civilization. Man is truly a "savage beast," endowed with powerful instinctive aggression; Freud challenged anyone, "in the face of all his experience of life and of history," to dispute this view (1961 [1930], 58–59).

Ego psychology has modified Freud's view somewhat, maintaining that the instinctual drives in human beings are not the same as those in animals, but that the concept of a drive is, rather, a construct which describes human conflict. It is a way of expressing opposing psychic structures that arise in the process of growth; the id no less than the ego is a product of such growth (Hartmann, Kris, Loewenstein, 89). In this theory, the id is a name for the conceptual locus of biological drives, as the ego is for the mechanisms of defense, and both are products of gradual differentiation. One of the functions of a culture is to provide spheres where the conflict between these two can be expressed without guilt (95). The nursery rhymes are one such sphere where the tendencies to cruelty may coexist with those to tenderness.

Cruelty to animals has long been associated with English culture. Keith Thomas has pointed out that between the sixteenth and eighteenth centuries, English children, especially boys, were often cited for their cruelty to animals, as in "Ding, dong, bell." Even a nineteenth-century illustration for this rhyme bluntly shows a boy throwing a cat into a well; the publication in 1833 of such an accompanying picture suggests a less squeamish view of such misdemeanors than we have today, for a modern illustrator would probably not depict it. (Figure 2) But such attitudes have persisted well into the twentieth century. In 1955, when Geoffrey Gorer published his study of the English national character, he quoted a number of answers to his query, "If you were told that a small child, say between 3 and 8, had done something really bad, what would you think the child had done?" Eighty-six percent of the respondents cited some type of aggression. And although Gorer does not comment on it, the majority of the answers he quotes as representative specifically mention cruelty to animals: "shut the cat/puppy in the oven," "done something to a dumb animal," "willfully ill-treated an animal," "probably been very cruel to an animal," "chopped a hen's head off," etc.

In England, bird scaring was historically a child's first employment, essential to the farmer at seedtime when the birds were a threat to freshly sown fields. (Opie, 83). Some rhymes seem designed to accompany this practical occupation:

> Away, bird, away,
> Take a little, and leave a little,
> And do not come again;
> For if you do,
> I will shoot you through,
> And there is an end of you. (no. 49)[1]

There are several other bird-killing rhymes, as well as several that refer to duck killing, or the sometime practical measure of clipping ducks' wings so they could not fly away when the time came to kill them. The little man with the gun and lead bullets, after shooting a "little duck, Right through the middle of the head, head head," vows he will have the drake as well, with no compunctions about overkill (no. 325), and an owl is fair game for a gunner, because it is "silly" or "stupid" (no. 393 and note).

Dogs and cats are also victimized without regret. The little maid in "Rowsty dowt," evidently in a temper, fed the truckler's dog and then knocked its head with the ladle, "And now poor Dapsy dog is dead" (no. 315). A lover suggests hanging his lady's dog to keep it from barking (no. 208), and because it has burned its tail, a little dog "must be hanged tomorrow" (no. 485). Barnaby Bright, once a good dog, will be hanged because he is "grown old and can no longer bark" (no. 33).[2] Mrs. Sheckleton killed Father Francis's cat because it stole a pound of butter—no doubt a serious offense; her only penance is to kiss the priest (no. 159).

Horses sometimes gain little sympathy as well. Several nags in the rhymes are lame or blind or both, but they are still expected to be serviceable to human needs:

> Will you lend me your mare to ride a mile?
> No, she is lame leaping over a stile.
> Alack! and I must go to the fair,
> I'll give you good money for lending your mare.
> Oh, oh! say you so?
> Money will make the mare to go. (no. 334)

And though the owner of the pony deplores such cruelty, it was a "lady" who whipped and slashed the pony and rode it "through the mire" (no. 127).

Such rhymes suggest that despite efforts to tidy up Mother Goose, sadistic drives remain powerful, even in the nursery. Several rhymes depict a certain amorality in children, especially toward animals.

> A little cock sparrow sat on a green tree,
> And he chirruped, he chirruped, so merry was he.
> A naughty boy came with his wee bow and arrow,
> Says he, I will shoot this little cock sparrow;
> His body will make me a nice little stew,
> And his giblets will make me a little pie too.
> Oh, no, said the sparrow, I won't make a stew,
> So he clapped his wings and away he flew. (no. 111)

Even more amorality pervades another rhyme, as it omits any comment about the sometimes serious consequences of shooting at birds:

> Robin-a-bobbin
> He bent his bow,
> Shot at a pigeon
> And killed a crow;
> Shot at another,
> And killed his own brother,

Did Robin-a-bobbin
Who bent his bow. (no. 449)

The Opies note that a version of "Robin-a-bobbin" is a chant for a
follow-the-leader game; it ends, "Shoot again, and kill a wren, and
that will do for gentlemen" (Opie, 371).[3]

Dogs in the rhymes sometimes represent servants, and become
targets of physical cruelty:

> I had a little dog, and his name was Blue Bell,
> I gave him some work, and he did it very well;
> I sent him up stairs to pick up a pin,
> He stepped in the coal-scuttle up to his chin;
> I sent him to the garden to pick some sage,
> He tumbled down and fell in a rage;
> I sent him to the cellar, to draw a pot of beer,
> He came up again and said there was none there. (no. 56)

> I had a little dog and they called him Buff,
> I sent him to a shop to buy me snuff,
> But he lost the bag and spilt the stuff;
> I sent him no more but gave him a cuff,
> For coming home from the mart without any snuff. (no. 83)

As we saw in *The Juvenile Cabinet* from 1806, uselessness was the
worst fault for an animal. In the human social structure, the same
obtains; what could be more useless than a useless servant? In other
rhymes, servants are thieves and lascivious laggards (nos. 310, 316,
477 in Opie). The suggestion is that servants have basically animal
natures, which necessitate their lower social status and the need for
controlling them.

Economist John Pullen has offered a Marxist critique of nursery
rhymes, in which he cites what he calls the "Margery Daw law." In
the famous seesaw rhyme (no. 335), Jack will be given a new master,
without any consultation with Jack, and he can make only a "penny
a day, Because he can't work any faster." Pullen comments:

> The reason for this wage cut is not because he is a troublemaker, or a
> shop steward, or because he is unwilling to work faster, but simply
> because he can't work any faster. He is to be punished because of his
> lack of innate ability. He is underprivileged and therefore must suffer.
> (58)

Such rhymes do more to propagate the capitalist system and laissez-
faire than all the economic theorists put together, according to

Pullen. It is because of them that the Jacks of the future accept their penny a day without questioning. Pullen does not cite animal rhymes in his 1979 article, but they seem to support his thesis. Indeed, dogs, which in the rhymes represent the lower orders of society, are subject to more gratuitous physical cruelty than other animals in the rhymes.[4]

Naughty or useless animals/servants also seem to represent children in the rhymes; their acts are childish—falling down, breaking things, general disobedience—and their punishments are the same as those meted out to children—being cuffed and denied food. No. 114 in the Opie collection originally referred to servants:

> Come when you're called,
>   Do as you're bid,
> Shut the door after you,
>   Never be chid. (no. 114)

The Opies speculate that this rhyme was "first turned on children" by the famous late-eighteenth-century novelist Maria Edgeworth, noted also for children's stories (Opie, 136). That it has remained in nursery rhyme books suggests that children and servants must observe the same standards of behavior. Geoffrey Gorer's exploration of English character supports the equation. He found that the concept of privilege dominated his respondents' answers on the subject of disciplining children; their comments suggested to him that "children's enjoyments are not 'rights,' but are granted by the benevolence of the parents while the child's conduct is satisfactory, and may be withdrawn under provocation" (Gorer, 187). Such an attitude certainly parallels that of employers toward servants, and further suggests a recognition that the baser natures of dogs and servants are the same as those of children—indeed of all of us, before those base natures are brought under control.

Further, Gorer found a pervasive and occasionally disturbing interest in what he called "the moral duty of punishing children and the pleasures of severity" (176). A large number of his respondents believed in corporal punishment, and some were remarkably original in its application (such as the father who forced his daughter to beat him with his belt, ostensibly to demonstrate that her lying hurt her parents [Gorer, 197]). Gorer noted the consistent use of the metaphor of pruning for disciplining children, with its implications of the imposition of physical punishment to create moral rectitude; he speculated that English may be the only European language that uses the same word for the place where plants and children are reared: *nursery* (Gorer, 163).

Ego psychology distinguishes between two kinds of behavior: institutionalized and noninstitutionalized. Here, the term *institution* is used in its widest, anthropological sense, as meaning a pattern of behavior that is important in the life of a given community. Institutionalized behavior is that which fits into such a pattern; it is conventional, preferred, accepted by the group as a whole. Noninstitutionalized behavior does not fit these patterns. Generally, classical psychoanalysis has tended to focus on noninstitutionalized behavior and its meaning, such as excessive hand washing or severe agoraphobia as neurotic manifestations. Ego psychology prefers to focus on institutionalized behavior in its many forms. Child care practices, for example, reveal the wide variety of behaviors that our culture accepts. Spanking, while many may deplore it and avoid it completely, is generally acceptable in its milder forms, and even those who practice more violent or unusual forms of it—such as the father cited earlier—generally encounter little serious interference from others.

Noninstitutionalized behavior does exist, however, and many may have tendencies toward it, which they keep under control. Hartmann, Kris, and Loewenstein speculate that cultures offer pathways of discharge for such tendencies, generally on the margins of institutionalized behavior (110–12). Unconscious tendencies toward physical aggression, for example, might find outlets in football, target shooting, wrestling, or some other sport. Unconscious anger toward a child might find its outlet in rough play. A corollary to this notion is that the more opportunities a culture offers for such release, the more chances an individual has for resolving such unconscious internal conflict. Those nursery rhymes that associate together disobedient, useless, or "untamed" animals, servants, and children, may offer such an outlet for the feelings that individuals have about all three.

This dynamic appears even more clearly in the nursery rhymes describing birds. As noted earlier in this chapter, many rhymes depict cruelty to birds; they are preyed upon and shot without compunction. However, these rhymes coexist with a number of popular rhymes in which the birds excite considerable sympathy:

> Once I saw a little bird
>   Come hop, hop, hop,
> And I cried, Little bird,
>   Will you stop, stop, stop?
>
> I was going to the window
>   To say, How do you do?
> When he shook his little tail,
>   And away he flew. (no. 46)
>
> Little Robin Redbreast
>   Came to visit me;
> This is what he whistled,
>   Thank you for my tea. (no. 451)

Indeed, when one looks at the entire body of the rhymes, the most pervasive anthropomorphic efforts seem to be aimed at birds, especially *little* birds; wrens, sparrows, English robins. Throughout the rhymes, more consistently than any other species, they seem to be imbued with human feelings and to excite sympathy:

> The north wind doth blow,
> And we shall have snow,
> And what will poor robin do then?
>   Poor thing.
>
> He'll sit in a barn,
> And keep himself warm,
> And hide his head under his wing.
>   Poor thing. (no. 533)

Again, the preponderance of these species as subjects for rhymes can be partly explained by practical familiarity, but there are other possibilities. Birds are more unlike humans than many other species; Levi-Strauss suggests that it is this very separation that encourages the projection of human characteristics onto the birds:

> They are feathered, winged, oviparous, and they are also physically separated from human society by the element in which it is their privilege to move. As a result of this fact, they form a community which is independent of our own but, precisely because of this independence, appears to us like another society, homologous to that in which we live; birds love freedom; they build themselves homes in which they live a family life and nurture their young; they often

engage in social relations with other members of their species; and they communicate with them by acoustic means recalling articulated language. (1966, 204)

This may be one reason for the prevalence of birds in the rhymes. However, the focus on *little* birds also suggests a strong association with children. Their size and apparent weakness, coupled with their elusiveness and their ability to survive, create a kind of natural linkage between birds and children, and yet the coexistence of bird-shooting rhymes and "The north wind doth blow" suggests the mixed feelings about children that characterize English culture.

The earliest extant nursery rhyme book, printed in 1744, contains as its opening rhyme a version of "Little Robin Redbreast," which, by virtue of its appearing in the book, must have been much older:

Little Robin Redbreast
Sitting on a pole.
Niddle, Noddle,
Went his head,
And Poop went his hole. (B-G, no. 1)

This crude little rhyme adopts a rather practical, observational attitude toward the bird, and as long as it remained oral only, was enjoyed as just that. But after its appearance in print, editors quickly tidied it up:

Little Robin Redbreast sat on a rail.
Niddle noddle went his head,
Wiggle waggle went his tail. (B-G, no. 26)

From a structuralist perspective, it was as if human identification with the bird could not be too physical; the separateness was essential for the symbol to work and for the sympathy to exist. From the point of view of ego psychology, the revision of the rhyme represents a revision of animality—the imposition of control on an instinctual drive. The message of such a revision is that taught to all children in a given culture: self-control.

The nursery rhymes that speak kindly of farm animals and pets, standing alongside those that express cruel tendencies, reinforce the notion that social control begins with self-control. Like child care practices, the raising of animals for human survival and consumption is an outgrowth of those primary institutions identified by Kardiner as basic to a culture. Pet keeping, in turn, is a secondary institution—in fact a relatively late development in English culture.

There are, of course, a number of hens, cows, and sheep throughout the rhymes. They tend, on the whole, to be treated tenderly and to make their owners proud of their generous natures. Milking rhymes especially, in their effort to charm the milk from the cow, show this tenderness:

> Cushy cow, bonny, let down thy milk,
> And I will give thee a gown of silk (no. 116)

> Hickety, pickety, my black hen,
> She lays eggs for gentlemen;
> Gentlemen come every day
> To see what my black hen doth lay. (no. 209)

It is not surprising to find that the vast majority of these animals in the rhymes are female. The term *hen* was in fact used in the seventeenth and eighteenth centuries for "woman" or "dear creature" (Opie, 202):

> I had a little hen,
>   The prettiest ever seen;
> She washed up the dishes,
>   And kept the house clean. (no. 210)

These animals slip into symbols of loving, generous wives and mothers, easily and happily domesticated.

Of course, the most famous maternal figure in the rhymes is Mother Goose herself. The association of geese, maternity, and folk rhymes and tales is shadowy and ancient; it may have begun with the mother of Charlemagne, who was called *La Reine Pedauque*, "Queen Goosefoot," or perhaps with the wife of Robert II of France, who from an incestuous union may have given birth to a creature with the head of a goose (Baring-Gould, 16–19). Certainly the association of maternity, the animal estate, and mysterious powers occurs in folklore and ritual worldwide; Levi-Strauss has explored it with regard to the South American opossum, prefacing his discussion of the animals symbolic function in Indian myth by a quotation from a French fabulist citing the opossum as a "model mother," whose "gentle, touching care, and maternal affection cannot fail to appeal to the reader" (1969, 164–95). The famous ladybird insect, which is urged to fly away home to save its child (no. 296 in Opie), is still used for divination, and the rhyme may be "a relic of something once possessed of an awful significance" (Opie, 263–64). Human maternity is the very type of cultural contradiction: on the one hand, a completely physiological event, messy, smelly, essential for survival; and on the other hand, a transcendent mystery fraught with hidden and overwhelming significance. Geese, too, excite ambivalent feelings: they combine an earthbound life with the ability to swim and fly; they may be tamed as pets and give their quills and feathers for human comfort. One rhyme expresses this tender maternal generosity:

> Cackle, cackle, Mother Goose,
> Have you any feathers loose?
> Truly have I, pretty fellow,
> Half enough to fill a pillow,
> Here are quills, take one or two,
> And down to make a bed for you. (no. 363)

Another rhyme seems to touch on Mother Goose's mysterious power to fly, but associates it with a male, and probably with sexual union:

> Old Mother Goose,
>   When she wanted to wander,
> Would ride through the air
>   On a very fine gander. (no. 364)

One is tempted to speculate that this rhyme attempts to contain the mysterious maternal power by making Mother Goose rely on a gander for her flight. The next chapter will explore this pattern in other rhymes. Here, it is offered as evidence for the complexity of the Mother Goose image. Geese, of course, can also be both stupid (for example, the popular insult of calling someone a goose) and aggressive. In all, with the usual remarkable aptness of folklore, such an image as Mother Goose is well suited to represent the dynamic cultural and psychological complexity of motherhood, and of the nursery rhymes themselves.

Pigs occupy a peculiar place in the rhymes. They are frequently associated with wearing wigs, partly, of course, because of the rhyme but also because the English seem to have found this image funny since it suggests a metaphoric insult to pretentious gentlemen. A more persistent association is that of pigs and feet; the toe-counting rhyme "This little pig went to market" (no. 412) is but one of several. Moreover, the rhymes distinguish between pigs and hogs, the latter more associated with adults and with distaste:

The pettitoes are little feet,
    And the little feet not big;
Great feet belong to the grunting hog,
    And the pettitoes to the little pig. (no. 408)

Such a complex of associations does not lend itself easily to interpretation. Certainly there is the suggestion of something low and
dirty in the linkage of feet and pigs; the persistent association of pigs
with children's feet, and especially with counting, is more subtle,
and seems to be part of an educational process.

On the other hand, the rhymes may also reflect pigs' peculiar
status in their relationship with humans. They seem as useless as
pet dogs, and like dogs they scavenge. Yet dogs are made pets, and
pigs are verbally abused as "filthy." The English are horrified at the
idea of eating dogs, yet they eagerly consume and enjoy pork. Edmund Leach speculates that human beings, especially those in English culture, feel a special guilt toward pigs:

> We rear pigs for the sole purpose of killing and eating them, and this is
> rather a shameful thing, a shame which quickly attaches to the pig
> itself. Besides which, under English rural conditions, the pig in his
> backyard sty was, until very recently, much more nearly a member of
> the household than any of the other edible animals. Pigs, like dogs,
> were fed from the leftovers of their human masters' kitchens. To kill
> and eat such a commensal associate is sacrilege indeed! (162)[5]

James Serpell in his study of pet keeping also cites pigs as a special
instance, in this case of the effects of modern agribusiness on a
species. The pig, raised in an entirely artificial environment, has
been "reduced to the status of a strictly utilitarian object" (1986, 6).
The shame that Leach describes hardly exists anymore, according to
Serpell, because few of us ever see pigs; and when we eat them, they
are neatly packaged in plastic wrap and labeled "pork," not "pig."
Thus our sensibilities are protected. Serpell's argument is that love
of and care for animals is a natural human characteristic, but since it
must coexist with our harsh treatment of economically useful species, we have developed a kind of split sensibility toward animals;
lavishing extravagant attentions on our domestic pets allows us to
manipulate other species without guilt (186).

Although Serpell does not mention it, the humorous use of pigs in
other forms of popular culture—cartoons, television shows, and so
on—is further evidence of this split. Making a pig a pet or using it to

symbolize a narcissistic woman is more amusing than using another species in this way, because of this underlying perception of the species as low and dirty, and because our guilt about our use of it can find an outlet in laughter, just as it does in the rhymes. At any rate, the symbolic function of the pig in the rhymes is a complex issue that will be further addressed in a later chapter.

Unlike the pig, the cat, although it too appears in many guises in the rhymes, has a clear symbolic function: it represents the archetypal female. This is an ancient association, of course, beginning at least with the Egyptian worship of cats as symbols of maternity, fecundity, and pleasure. Throughout the rhymes, cats are associated with home and hearth, with women in the household, and with children. However, they also prey on mice and birds and are untrustworthy, amoral, and occasionally dangerous:

> I've been to market, my lady, my lady;
> Then you've not been to the fair, says pussy, says pussy.
> I bought me a rabbit, my lady, my lady;
> Then you did not buy a hare, says pussy, says pussy.
> I roasted it, my lady, my lady.
> Then you did not boil it, says pussy, says pussy.
> I eat it, my lady, my lady;
> And I'll eat you, says pussy, says pussy. (no. 292)

Harriet Ritvo found the cat the "most frequently and energetically vilified domestic animal" throughout nineteenth-century English rhetoric (21). But the rhymes do not seem to vilify cats so much as to find them mysterious and in need of control. The cat in the rhymes is both maternal and potentially murderous. The mother of the three little kittens encourages good behavior such as washing and eating all one's dinner, but becomes a predator when she smells a succulent rat close by. The cat and kittens in "A frog he would a-wooing go" (no. 175) break up the merrymaking without warning, killing the sociable Mr. Rat and Mrs. Mouse; Randolph Caldecott depicted this mother cat in a ruffled dress as she makes her deadly pounce (Figure 3).

Dogs in the rhymes, by contrast, are often noisy and troublesome and, as mentioned earlier in this chapter, frequently suffer physical punishment. Some are beloved pets, however:

> Oh where, Oh where has my little dog gone?
> Oh where, oh where can he be?

The Cat she seized the Rat by the crown;
  Heigho, says ROWLEY!
The Kittens they pulled the little Mouse down.
  With a rowley-powley, gammon and spinach,
  Heigho, says ANTHONY ROWLEY!

Figure 3. Illustration by Randolph Caldecott from *A Frog He Would a-Wooing Go.* de Grummond Children's Literature Research Collection.

> With his ears cut short and his tail cut long,
>   Oh where, oh where is he? (no. 139)

Probably the most famous pet dog in English literature is Old Mother Hubbard's, who performs outrageous antics as his mistress attempts to serve him:

> She took a clean dish
>   To get him some tripe;
> But when she came back,
>   He was smoking a pipe.
>
> She went to the alehouse
>   To get him some beer;
> But when she came back,
>   The dog sat in a chair. (no. 365)

This rhyme is probably the single most famous and successful rhyme ever to be transmitted orally or in print. It first appeared in

1805, at the beginning of the century when pet keeping and the humane treatment of animals were beginning to take real hold in English life, and may be partially a barometer of this interest. The public seemed ravenous for more verses, and many were composed and printed anonymously; the Opies estimate that a new version of the rhyme has appeared each year since 1805 (Opie, 320). However, the wonderful dog is obviously much more than a pet to Mother Hubbard; he is, metaphorically speaking, her child, and yet, in his masculine activities, also a type of husband and master—certainly a reversal of the usual owner/pet relationship, as well as a reversal of the more common gender association of woman and cat. Indeed, "Old Mother Hubbard" is probably based on an earlier rhyme, "Dame Trot and her Comical Cat," a rhyme still known in England but which has never achieved the wider familiarity of "Mother Hubbard" (Opie, 320–21). With the shift from cat to dog, a clearer distinction between the male and female was established in the rhyme, a distinction that probably helps explain the rhyme's popularity. It speaks more to the relationship between the sexes, and to the relationship between mother and child than to that between humans and animals and will be discussed in more detail in the next chapter.

Another famous pet in the rhymes is Mary's lamb, which followed her everywhere, even waiting patiently at school:

> Why does the lamb love Mary so?
>   The eager children cry;
> Why, Mary loves the lamb, you know,
>   The teacher did reply. (no. 341)

This appears to be a relatively late rhyme, probably composed in 1830 and one of the few rhymes written by a single person—evidently Mrs. Sara Josepha Hale (though there have been other claimants; see Opie, 300). Thus, even more than "Old Mother Hubbard," this rhyme reflects the English public spirit during the early nineteenth century, when, in 1822, the Prevention of Cruelty to Animals Act was passed.

Harriet Ritvo in *The Animal Estate* (1987) has written a fascinating study of the rhetoric surrounding animals in England during this period. Her research treats a subject seldom addressed because so rooted in our unconscious attitudes, toward animals and toward each other. In so doing, it offers persuasive evidence of the dynamic interaction between institutionalized and noninstitutionalized behavior in English culture.

Ritvo begins where Keith Thomas leaves off, after the "profound shift in sensibilities" from cruelty to kindness (Thomas, 15) was completed in the late eighteenth century. During the nineteenth century, the English found animals not only lovable but also suitable subjects for manipulation and domination, and the rhetoric associated with them demonstrated how important they were in the "imaginative life of the most enthusiastically exploitative culture of the nineteenth century" (Ritvo, 6).

Ritvo has thoroughly examined the records establishing and continuing the Smithfield Club (devoted to cattle breeding), the Board of Agriculture, the British Kennel Club, the Royal Society for the Prevention of Cruelty to Animals, the antirabies movement, the London Zoo, and the codes surrounding big game hunting in the colonies. In every instance, she demonstrates persuasively that the language of these entities, though professing to be that of science, is really that of rank and morality.

For example, cattle are essential to English life, and one would assume that breeding them would enhance their usefulness. In fact, cattle breeding during the nineteenth century became the province of the elite, who even during periods of agricultural depression spent huge sums on the breeding of larger and larger animals, until sometimes the cattle were so fat as to be completely useless except as symbols of the power of their wealthy and manipulative breeders.[6] Such breeders stressed the importance of not mixing their animals with others of inferior blood, and "sensible farmers" were advised not to participate in such breeding, implying that they should know their place (54).

Ritvo demonstrates that the Kennel Club and the "dog and cat fancying establishments" were entirely the products of rhetoric. Standards were completely arbitrary, since, because these animals were strictly pets, no standards of usefulness applied. And unlike cattle breeding, dog and cat breeding was open to the middle classes; as the rhetoric surrounding these animals came to emphasize manipulation and rank by competition rather than association, the stock of well-descended animals rose, and that of the more common ones fell. Pet shows became a "respectable and well-ordered pastime, a reflection of the carefully calibrated human social order" (104).

The establishment of the RSPCA and the growth of the antirabies movement focused even more clearly on social rank. As the English came to deplore cruelty to animals, its control came to represent self-control; kindness to animals became a code for the acceptance of social responsibilities, and cruelty a code for deviance (132). Naturally, the lower social orders were the most deviant and the most in need of control; the records of the RSPCA documented case after case of cruelty to animals, all of which were perpetrated by the lower classes. "Thus the rhetoric of animal protection simultaneously isolated and stigmatized a large segment of the Victorian public" (136). In the panicky rhetoric surrounding rabies, the fear of which was entirely out of proportion to its actual incidence, the dogs of the poor were most to blame. (Ritvo points out that the fear of syphilis was similar, the disease being associated almost entirely with prostitutes—that is, almost any woman of low social status [186]). Dog licensing metaphorically identified and classified dog *owners*, once again establishing control over the lower classes.

Attitudes toward wild and exotic animals reflected the same concern. In the hierarchy of "good" and "bad" wild animals, only those that could be "persuaded at least partly to abandon their unregenerate state" received praise (22). Elephants were especially valued; two of them became public pets. Zoos generally demonstrated the imposition of order and control on the chaos of nature, and the bagging of wild game in the colonies, with its attendant image of the noble white hunter controlling both animal and human wildlife, demonstrated the march of empire, assumed to be an unqualified advantage to all concerned (254).

Though Ritvo seldom mentions it specifically, children's literature played an active part in all of this, especially in the inculcation of kindness toward animals as a representation of self-control. One of the rhymes in the Opie collection was directly occasioned by the passage of the 1822 act preventing cruelty to animals; Jacob Beuler took the first two lines of an old folk rhyme and developed them into one of the most popular songs of the century. Its nursery version is somewhat shorter but the message is the same:

> If I had a donkey that wouldn't go,
> Would I beat him? Oh no, no.
> I'd put him in the barn and give him some corn,
> The best little donkey that ever was born. (no. 142)

"Mary had a little lamb," "Ding, dong, bell," "I love little pussy," and many other rhymes suggest, not very subtly, that kindness and gentleness toward animals are desirable qualities.

The Baring-Goulds offer a version of the horse's prayer to its master, which they do not date but which must surely spring from the nineteenth century:

> Going up hill whip me not;
> Coming down hill hurry me not;
> On level ground spare me not;
> Loose in the stable forget me not;
> Of hay and corn rob me not;
> Of clean water stint me not;
> With sponge and water neglect me not;
> Of soft bed deprive me not;
> Tired and hot wash me not;
> If sick or cold chill me not;
> With bit or rein oh, jerk me not;
> And when you are angry strike me not. (B-G, no. 487)

It is psychologically interesting that the key word here is *not*. This emphasis on prohibition suggests that even neglectful activities may result from a conscious or unconscious intention to hurt. During this century, too, the famous novel *Black Beauty* (1877) was written, an "animal autobiography" by Anna Sewell, describing in painful detail not only cruelty to horses but the human degradations of drink and poverty. The book was a publishing success, selling many millions of copies, appearing in several languages, and firmly establishing itself as a children's classic. Sewell, a Quaker, was no doubt as gentle as her book begs others to be. But one is tempted to wonder, psychoanalytically speaking, if the popularity of such a book and of such rhymes—and indeed of the sometimes florid rhetoric that Ritvo describes—does not represent what is known in psychoanalytic parlance as reaction formation. In this form of defense, powerful drives such as aggression are kept under control by oversolicitous kindness and concern for others, even to the extent of completely repressing the drive itself (Waelder, 183). The stringent measures of control suggested by "Going uphill whip me not" certainly suggest an equally strong tendency toward aggression.

A minor but striking instance of the persistence of a powerful impulse is the occasional reference in the rhymes to bestiality. Zoophilia and bestiality appear in the myths of many cultures, not least the Greek myths with their centaurs, harpies, satyrs, and gods who became beasts in order to ravish humans. These stories continue to have a strong appeal despite the prohibitions against such behavior in cultures that acknowledge and enjoy the myths. Bestiality is specifically prohibited in Talmudic law and in the Old Testament, and Christianity regards it as one of the most heinous sexual crimes (Serpell, 27). It was made a capital offense in England in 1534, and at Tyburn, near London, in 1679, a woman and a dog were hanged together for the offense. One nursery rhyme toys with the notion:

> There was a lady loved a swine,
>   Honey, quoth she,
> Pig-hog wilt thou be mine?
>   Hoogh, quoth he.
>
> I'll build thee a silver sty
> . . . .
> Pinned with a silver pin
> . . . .
> Wilt thou have me now,
>   Honey? quoth she.
> Speak or my heart will break.
>   Hoogh, quoth he. (no. 294)

The English seem to have found this rhyme hilarious (one is also reminded of Titania's infatuation with Bottom as an ass in *A Midsummer-Night's Dream*). The configuration of a woman in love with an animal is one which, like "Old Mother Hubbard," speaks more to the relationship between the sexes than to that between human and animal. This rhyme will therefore be explored further in the next chapter. For now, the irony seems to be that the crime of bestiality is mentioned much more often than it has ever been committed; Keith Thomas notes that few instances of it are on record, in contrast to the number of moralists who mention it (118–19). This suggests that, like the prohibitions on cruelty to animals, the prohibition on bestiality exists to control a powerful and persistent human impulse.[7]

By acknowledging drives toward cruelty and bestiality, nursery rhymes about animals address the problem of *social* control through *self*-control, which is its origin and emblem. This is the same connection that prompted Freud to write *Totem and Taboo* (1913), where he advanced his famous notion of the primal crime. For Freud, the laws forbidding parricide and incest represent the beginning of culture—the first imposition by human beings of restrictions on their own behavior and the representations of those restrictions by symbols. In Freud's view, the strong aggressive and libidinal impulses in the human personality were directly responsible for culture, since they required limits and controls if human beings were to survive. Jealousy, rage, desire, anxiety, and guilt persist in all human beings. If they did not, no laws would be necessary to control them; the persistence of such laws is proof of the persistence of the impulse.

The shortcomings of Freud's venture into anthropology have been thoroughly explored (see especially Wallace, *Freud and Anthropology* [1983]); most of them center on his famous speculation about the murder and subsequent veneration of the primal father by his sons. But concern with this remarkable conjecture need not obscure the more solid elements of theory in the book. One is the emphasis on ambivalence in the notion of taboo. The word *taboo* has a double meaning now: "sacred" and "unclean." Freud notes that it originally meant "what may not be touched," a characteristic common to both extremes (66). In fact, Freud believes that the word was ambivalent from the beginning, and that the "prohibitions of taboo are to be understood as consequences of an emotional ambivalence" (67). For Freud, it is just such ambivalence that forces neurotics into their peculiar prohibitions; the Rat Man's ambivalence toward his dead father is only one example among many in Freud's canon.

Freud goes on in *Totem and Taboo* to explore the emotional ambivalence of children in their relationship with animals: "Children show no trace of the arrogance which urges adult civilized men to draw a hard-and-fast line between their own nature and that of all other animals. Children have no scruples over allowing animals to rank as their full equals" (127). However, children often develop severe phobias about animals, which Freud believes represent the child's fear of its parents. He cites his own case of Little Hans, and Ferenczi's case of Little Arpad, as evidence of such displacement; the love and admiration for the parent coupled with fear and rivalry produce an ambivalence that can find its outlet only in a phobia— one of the principle characteristics of which is a strong identification with the animal the child fears. Such a phobia is one manifestation of the Oedipus complex, which is itself the result of the imposition of control on the child's drives. The self-control that characterizes kindness to animals is metaphorically the self-control with which the child controls its desire for one parent and identifies with the other. What is most important is that the drives to destroy and to possess are still present; they have only been tamed into a configuration that is acceptable to society.

English nursery rhymes, with their deep ambivalence toward animals, carry messages to children about the necessity of such self-control. The messages recognize the power and persistence of the drives to cruelty and violence; at the same time they address the need for controlling those drives. Such messages represent hard-won wisdom, coming from adults who have grappled with the same drives and only partially tamed them.

It is significant that the animals in the rhymes are almost entirely *domestic* animals—emblems of nature tamed. Wild animals are classic symbols of untamed id impulses, such as the silent white wolves in the most famous dream of Freud's most famous patient. Wild animals are

> life unmitigated by complexities of consciousness, language, ethics, treachery, revulsion, reason, religions, premeditation or free will. A wild animal does not contradict its own nature, does not thwart itself, as man endlessly does. A wild animal never plays for the other side. The wild animals are a holiday from deliberation. They are sheer life. (Morrow, unpaged)

Alan Dundes has speculated on the function of projection in circuses, suggesting that since the wish to be like a wild animal is a guilty one for human adults, they project and invert this wish onto animals, thus imagining that the animal wishes to be human (1980, 56). Certainly the spectacle of caged wild animals suggests the caging of our own animal natures, as well as the constant danger that those natures could escape. The nursery rhymes offer few examples of this spectacle, however, choosing to focus almost entirely on the tamed and domestic animal. This focus suggests that the rhymes, as a cultural institution, represent the triumph of the defenses: nature can indeed be tamed.

In civilization, human beings must learn to deliberate, contradict, premeditate, and reason, though their impulses often weigh against it. The defenses we erect to control such impulses may vary individually, but in many ways they are also prescribed by the culture. Edwin Wallace (1983), in his excellent study of Freud's *Totem and*

Taboo, notes that the educational process is the "crucial factor" determining the individual's use of defense mechanisms, especially archaic ones such as projection or omnipotence of thoughts (223). The nursery rhymes, then, might be seen as "institutionalized projections," in Wallace's term, useful in alleviating conflicts in centuries of children because the same conflicts and ambivalences have bedeviled them for centuries. As cultural institutions, these animal rhymes offer the dual comforts of understanding and control: they understand the drives, and do not deny their existence, but they also offer the means of control. Keith Thomas believes that toy animals, on which children can lavish extravagant love and care, represent "fantasies which enshrine the values by which society as a whole cannot afford to live" (301). The nursery rhymes about animals are fantasies by which society does indeed live.

There was a little man,
And he wooed a little maid,
And he said, Little maid, will you wed, wed, wed?
I have little more to say,
Than will you, yea or nay?
For the least said is soonest mended, ded, ded.

Then this little maid she said,
Little sir, you've little said,
To induce a little maid for to wed, wed, wed;
You must say a little more,
And produce a little ore,
Ere I to the church will be led, led, led.

CHAPTER 3 **Wooing and Wedding**

The Relationship

between the Sexes

The rhymes describing men and women, and their interaction
through courtship and marriage, comprise the largest group explored
in this study. Finding ways to express the relationship between the
sexes—and ways to control it—is an abiding interest in any culture,
since in that relationship lies the culture's hope for preservation. It
may be surprising to find that the rhymes reflect less romance than
hardheaded practicality, but such attitudes reveal the pattern of individual choice, combined with an eye to the market value of the
married state, that especially distinguishes English culture. The
rhymes reveal a deeper psychological pattern as well: fear of woman—that powerful, mysterious, loving, threatening figure that dominates human infancy. It is probably no accident, finally, that these
are called *Mother* Goose rhymes.

Many cultures express this fear of woman in the archetype of the
phallic woman. One theory suggests that this archetype is based on
an ontogenetically earlier question of breast with penis, and may

Figure 4. Illustration by Walter Crane from
The Baby's Opera. de Grummond Children's
Literature Research Collection.

express unconscious oral desires connected with earliest childhood (Kiell, 53). Whatever its origins, its representations in art vary from figures of women with breasts and phalluses found in preliterate tribes, to murderous women in literature such as Clytemnestra and Lady Macbeth, to the modern stereotype of the executive woman, all sharing the characteristic of power. In these artistic representations, their power is revealed in their bodies, their actions, or their clothing. In life, however, as psychoanalysis suggests, women's power is more concealed and mysterious. Karen Horney addressed this issue in a famous paper, "The Dread of Woman," in which she speculated on men's anxiety regarding the hidden female genital; this anxiety "weighs more heavily, and is usually more energetically repressed than the dread of man (father) . . . the endeavor to find the penis in women represents first and foremost a convulsive attempt to deny the existence of the sinister female genital" (1967 [1932], 138). In this paper she confined her discussion to the male's dread of the female, but a year earlier, she had noted that a man's dread of women was more associated with the fear of death than was a woman's dread of men, and had commented, "It is as though we are possessed by the idea that the one who gives life is also capable of taking it away" (1967 [1931] 117). Thus young children of both genders experience this archetypal fear, since they are literally dependent on a woman for their survival.

The archetype of the phallic woman in the rhymes takes many forms.[1] One manifestation is the coy milkmaid. Milkmaids are stock figures in the rhymes, responding to suggestions that they be accompanied on their milking duties with sly good humor:

Little maid, pretty maid, whither goest thou?
  Down in the forest to milk my cow.
Shall I go with thee? No, not now.
  When I send for thee, then come thou. (no. 313)

Where are you going to, my pretty maid?
I'm going a-milking, sir, she said. . . .

What is your fortune, my pretty maid?
My face is my fortune, sir, she said.
Then I can't marry you, my pretty maid.
Nobody asked you, sir, she said. (no. 317)

This latter rhyme is a bowdlerized version of a much older one in which the maid responds matter-of-factly that she will bear the suitor's child after he "lays her down upon the ground." And some versions have as the refrain, "It's rolling in the dew makes the milkmaids fair." The Opies suggest that this refers to the belief that dew is good for the complexion, but this seems a genteel displacement from the sexual activity implied by "rolling" (Opie, 282–85). Asking to accompany a milkmaid on her milking was the equivalent of proposing marriage (Opie, 280), but "marriage" seems in these rhymes a euphemism for copulation, and the whole configuration of milkmaid/forest/suitor a metaphor for sexual activity with any flirtatious but willing girl. That they should so often be milkmaids, however, with the accompanying associations of the cow's anatomy and the activity of milking, suggests that they may also be mother-figures, associated unconsciously with infantile hunger and satisfaction and expressing the breast-penis equation mentioned earlier. These phallic women express their power in their mysterious ability to give food from their own bodies; their coyness further suggests their ability to withhold that desired food.

The darker aspect of the phallic woman who gives food informs one very famous rhyme:

> Where have you been today, Billy, my son?
> Where have you been today, my only man?
> I've been a wooing, mother, make my bed soon,
> For I'm sick at heart, and fain would lay down.
> What have you ate today, Billy, my son?
> What have you ate today, my only man?
> I've ate eel-pie, mother, make my bed soon,
> For I'm sick at heart, and shall die before noon. (no. 44)

The Opies provide lengthy notes on this rhyme, calling it "perhaps the last living (i.e. still orally transmitted) link with a tale possibly terrible in origin and certainly mysterious in its subsequent history" (Opie, 76). The woman Billy has courted has affinities with all the fatal women since Eve; she is a prime example of the dangerous phallic woman, even to serving eels, an old and classic phallic symbol, in almost every known version of the rhyme. Nursery rhyme collector James O. Halliwell speculated in 1849 that Billy might have been "visited by his mermaid mother" (Baring-Gould, 169). This figure is balanced in the rhyme by Billy's human mother, loving and concerned, calling him her "only man." This rhyme thus depicts two archetypal mothers wanting possession of Billy; the fatal woman wins, as Billy forfeits his life—the ultimate castration, the ultimate price for involvement with such a woman.

Some women in the rhymes possess rather obvious phallic substitutes:

Hannah Bantry, in the pantry,
Gnawing at a mutton bone;
  How she gnawed it,
  How she clawed it,
When she found herself alone. (no. 203)

The masturbatory theme seems obvious, but it takes a masculine form with the "bone." Another old woman has mysterious powers in her broom:

There was an old woman tossed up in a basket,
Seventeen times as high as the moon;
Where she was going I couldn't but ask it,
For in her hand she carried a broom.
Old woman, old woman, old woman, quoth I,
Where are you going to up so high?
To brush the cobwebs off the sky!
May I go with you?
Aye, by-and-by. (no. 545)

One of the most repellent and threatening images of the phallic woman in the rhymes appears in an unexpected context. The Baring-Gould collection prints several extra verses to "What are little boys made of," besides the famous first two. The verses treat, in order, little boys, little girls, young men, young women, old women, sailors, and soldiers. Old *men* are conspicuously omitted, and the verse describing old women has not only phallic implications but those of the *vagina dentata* as well—a term that describes the folk suspicion that the vagina is "toothed" and hence castrating:

What are old women made of?
  Bushes and thorns
  And old cow's horns,
That's what old women are made of. (B-G, no. 320)[2]

Such a variety of mothers/women, combining nurturing with threat, wielding their mysterious powers to feed, wound, and kill, well expresses the flexibility of the archetype, as well as the deep fears that engender it. Kleinian theory proposes that every child harbors, as a consequence of total dependency, the dread that the mother may poison it or otherwise destroy it, a dread that both engenders and coexists with anger and aggression toward the object—the mother. The child's aggression projected outward causes the mother to appear threatening and protects the child from its own aggression, which is genuinely dangerous and doubly frightening, since it threatens the child's own survival. The pervasive presence of the archetype of the fatal woman in the rhymes (to say nothing of her appearance in countless other forms of literature and art) strongly testifies to its presence in the human unconscious and to its infantile origins.

English culture shares its fear of women with many others, and like many others, has found ways to control that fear, which have become embedded in the social structure. One of the most famous nursery rhymes offers an image of such control:

> Peter, Peter, pumpkin eater,
> Had a wife and couldn't keep her;
> He put her in a pumpkin shell
> And there he kept her very well. (no. 405)

"Keep" here carries the meaning of "provide for," and suggests that Peter was a practical man who used his resources cleverly. But the image of the wife in the enclosed shell certainly implies "keep" in the more sinister modern sense (sinister even when the "shell" is an elegant suburban home). In a patriarchal culture, in which males have positions of public power and women occupy the domestic sphere, such a division of labor allows both men and women to contain their deep unconscious fear of women's ultimate and mysterious procreative power, at the same time protecting it and ensuring its usefulness to the community.

Categorization, overvaluation, and devaluation are defenses every culture offers its inhabitants. The act of categorizing is that of separating and drawing boundaries; Levi-Strauss has attempted to show that it is an essential feature of human thought, part of the very process of thinking itself. It offers a way of controlling the chaotic flow of experience and surroundings, and though it may be finally illusory, it offers comfort as well. For example, placing women in categories such as virgin or widow is an act of symbolic containment, offering the illusion that their powers are contained and hence no longer threatening. Assigning value is also a central act of culture, part of its very definition and a notorious intercultural variable: what one culture overvalues, another denigrates, and vice versa. Courtship, for example, an institution which results from assigning value to potential marriage partners, hardly exists in most societies (Macfarlane, 293); English courtship is unusual in its emphasis on individual choice and compatibility, which other cultures find repellent since such attitudes value the individual above the group. Value is thus more easily perceived as illusory than categories, but without it no culture could maintain itself. It too is a defense against the surrounding chaos of items and events, and of men and women, who may be highly valued or cast aside according to the culture's standards of marriageability.

The relationship between the sexes is an area in which one can see, in any given culture, these three defenses in operation, for in marriage customs they combine to regulate and perpetuate the social order. Men and women are categorized, overvalued, or devalued according to their perceived ability to contribute to the culture's stability; even in a patriarchal culture, both sexes take part in these ways of perceiving each other, and generally acknowledge their usefulness. English nursery rhymes reflect these defenses offered by English culture—defenses that persist to a remarkable degree today, despite the level of social change, because they acknowledge powerful impulses while offering the means to control them. That there should be so many nursery rhymes exploring the relationship between the sexes should come as no surprise; such rhymes address themselves to children's intense interest in the relationship between the sexes, and to the most crucial interest of culture: its perpetuation.

Throughout the rhymes, and indeed throughout other kinds of literature, women are much more subject to rigid categorization than men. However, the depictions of men in the rhymes offer an image that tends to unify them as well: they are almost invariably pictured as social beings, acting in public settings and enjoying each other's company.

Probably the most famous man in the rhymes, besides the man in the moon, is Old King Cole, the merry old soul:

> And a merry old soul was he;
> He called for his pipe,

And he called for his bowl,
And he called for his fiddlers three. (no. 112)

There are other drinkers and smokers among the rhymes as well. "A little fat man of Bombay" enjoys his pipe until a bird steals it away (no. 61); the grenadier has spent all his money on drink and can't be admitted to the pub (no. 196). "Old Boniface" loves good cheer and good drink (no. 63); his name became a label for all public-house keepers (Opie, 92). In "Over the water and over the lea," Charley loves good ale, wine, and brandy as much as he loves a girl (no. 96). Even the man in the moon gets advice about his tipple:

> The man in the moon drinks claret,
> But he is a dull jack-a-dandy;
> Would he know a sheep's head from a carrot
> He should learn to drink cider and brandy. (no. 332)

During the sixteenth and seventeenth centuries, when these rhymes and others like them were probably first composed, drunkenness was extremely common. A study of rural life in Wessex shows that by far the greatest number of entries for court records concern "unlicensed tippling houses, excessive drinking, drunkenness, unlawful gaming at alehouses . . . . these problems even outnumber the entries on bastardy or the care of paupers" (Bettey, 61). Even church functions were not exempt from such disorder; in 1617 one Harry Spinter was drunk in church, and, before evening prayer, went up into the tower "and at a trappe dore did piss downe upon theare heads in the belfrey that they could not stand there nor neare to itt to the great offence of those that were present" (quoted in Bettey, 61). The author of this history speculates that the tedium and harshness of life as well as a monotonous diet led to such excesses; women, however, were subject to at least as much harshness, tedium, and poor food, but the common drunk was almost exclusively male, and certainly in areas and times of less harshness and tedium, alehouses have flourished. A likelier explanation is the social nature of drinking, especially for men.

Several rhymes depict men enjoying each other's company: the three wise men of Gotham (no. 192), the three jovial Welshmen (no. 525), and the famous three men in a tub (no. 460). The Opies suggest that these latter three men are probably not merely enjoying innocent companionship; the earliest versions of the rhyme depict the butcher, baker, and candlestick maker watching three *maids* in a tub at a fair—that is, they have gone to a "dubious side-show," no place for respectable gentlemen but fun nonetheless, and the kind of fun men enjoy with each other (Opie, 376). The persistence of the number 3 in these rhymes reinforces these men's sociability: one is solitary, two are companionable, but three are sociable. Other male-perpetrated infractions in the rhymes are also sociable, at least in the sense that they are not solitary. Taffy the Welshman and thief gets into a rivalry with the narrator to see who can do the other the most irritating injury:

Taffy was a Welshman, Taffy was a sham;
Taffy came to my house and stole a leg of lamb;
I went to Taffy's house. Taffy was away,
I stuffed his socks with sawdust and filled his shoes with clay. (no.
495)

"Charley, Charley" (no. 95) steals from the baker. "Little Tom Tittlemouse" ostensibly steals "fishes from other men's ditches," though a transformation in this rhyme suggests that he may be stealing sex instead: plucking out fishes from hidden places may be a metaphor for sexual activity. (See Baring-Gould, 29, 31.) Whipping, sometimes known as *"la vice Anglaise,"* is also a kind of social crime practiced among males, especially in academic settings; the nursery rhyme version takes it for granted:

Doctor Faustus was a good man,
He whipped his scholars now and then;
When he whipped them he made them dance
Out of Scotland into France,
Out of France into Spain,
And then he whipped them back again. (no. 162)

This is an 1842 version; earlier English versions, with other names for the doctor, still maintain, though perhaps ironically, that he is "nice" or "good" (Opie, 168).

Considerably fewer rhymes depict *old* men than depict old women, but several of those suggest that the old men are sexually interested if not active:

There was an old man in a velvet coat,
He kissed a maid and gave her a groat;
The groat was cracked and would not go,
Ah, old man, do you serve me so? (no. 329)

Walter Crane, a frequent illustrator of the rhymes, seemed to sense this pattern; in his illustration for "Where are you going to, my pretty maid" in *The Baby's Opera*, he depicted, instead of a young suitor for the saucy maid, a relatively old man (Figure 4). And the unfortunate old man who would not say his prayers was found in "my lady's chamber" (no. 190).

All of these rhymes depict men in social or sexual situations, no matter what their age or status, and unlike the rhymes depicting women, most of that social activity is among men. An extra verse of "If all the world were paper" (no. 548) dating from 1641, wonders:

> If all the World were men,
> And men lived all in trenches,
> And there were none but we alone
> How should we doe [sic] for Wenches.

The Opies point out, though, that this verse appears only once, in a manuscript miscellany (Opie, 437). That this verse never became popular suggests that the idea of a world exclusively of men might not be something to bemoan after all. When Crane illustrated this rhyme, this verse did not appear but his illustration showed men smoking and toasting each other.

Men's relationships with their fathers occupy a handful of the rhymes, most of which represent the father as dead and the son as inheriting:

> My father died a month ago,
> And left me all his riches;
> A feather bed, and a wooden leg,
> And a pair of leather breeches. (no. 155)

> My father he died, but I can't tell you how,
> He left me six horses to drive in my plough. (no. 156)

> My father he left me, just as he was able,
> One bowl, one bottle, one table,
> Two bowls, two bottles, two tables
> Three bowls . . . (no. 157)

> My father left me three acres of land,
> Sing ivy, sing ivy;
> My father left me three acres of land,
> Sing holly, go whistle and ivy! (no. 158)

One of the peculiarities of English culture, according to anthropological historian Alan Macfarlane, is the flow of goods and property downward rather than upward. The majority of societies transmit wealth from children to parents, making it desirable to sire a large number of children. In England, property descends from parents to children, making a small number of children a more rational choice (Macfarlane, 72). Nursery rhymes suggest not only that pattern but a pattern in which wealth is concentrated in the hands of men:

> Clap hands, clap hands,
>   Till father comes home;
> For father's got money,
>   But mother's got none. (no. 200)

The owner of the jolly sixpence lets his money dwindle away until he has nothing to take home to his wife (no. 480), and even a man who "had nought" is pursued by robbers (no. 320).

Plenty of male companionship, plenty of drink, sexual interests well into old age, money and possessions rightfully his, outlets for aggression, and a deceased father: these are the oedipal male fantasies that inform these rhymes.[3] They tend to depict men without too much categorizing, and to define them against each other. In contrast, women in the rhymes are most often categorized by their relationships to men just as they are in society: they are young and awaiting marriage, middle-aged and married, or old and seemingly widowed.

The passivity that is often associated with the nubile young girl in other forms of literature and that English society does seem to enjoin upon her, is the focus of a few rhymes. The girl who loves "Bobby Shafto" simply waits for him to return and marry her (no. 60); the girl in the famous folk song "O dear, what can the matter be?" waits at home for her Johnny, who has been "too long at the fair" (Opie, 248). The duties of the girl about to be married mostly involve powdering and curling her hair while she waits for her love (no. 464). The Baring-Goulds associate "Around the green gravel" with the promenade of eligible maidens around the village green while the young men look over the crop and select a wife from among them (B-G, no. 326). Chapter 12 of the Baring-Gould collection, "Mother Goose's Charms," contains a number of love charms supposedly employed by young girls to discover who their future lovers are:

> If you find a hairpin,
> Stick it in your shoe;
> The next boy you talk with
> Is sure to marry you. (B-G, no. 500)

> Make a rhyme, make a rhyme,
> See your beau before bedtime. (B-G, no. 513)

The most famous and long-lasting of such charms is probably the daisy one, in which one pulls the petals from a daisy while reciting, "He loves me, he loves me not." These rhymes provide a kind of activity for the otherwise passive girl waiting for marriage; they also suggest that interest in whom she will marry permeates most of her waking and sleeping thoughts.

Other women are less than passive, but still more interested in getting a man than anything else:

> I am a pretty wench,
> And I come a great way hence,
> And sweethearts I can get none:
> But every dirty sow
> Can get sweethearts enough,
> And I pretty wench can get none. (no. 526)

> Trip upon trenchers, and dance upon dishes,
> My mother sent me for some barm, some barm;
> She bid me tread lightly, and come again quickly,
> For fear the young men should do me some harm.
> Yet didn't you see, yet didn't you see,
> What naughty tricks they put upon me:
> They broke my pitcher,
> And spilt the water,
> And huffed my mother,
> And chid her daughter,
> And kissed my sister instead of me. (no. 520)

"Barm" is the yeasty foam that rises to the top of fermenting malt liquors; yeast is also a common symbol of female sexual activity as implied by an earlier version of this rhyme, which says that the girl, on her errand, met first the lord of the manor who could do her no harm:

> But down in the park, I met with the clerk,
> And he gied me my barm, my barm! (Opie, 417)

There are several interesting transformations here: furtive copulation (perhaps even a rape?) is replaced by rowdy, violent, but social
behavior on the part of the men, and the girl as victim is replaced by
the girl as a rather foolish, jealous creature who probably wouldn't
mind the rowdy behavior if the men had kissed her rather than
another.

The rhymes also have their share of prostitutes. "Little Blue Betty" (no. 57) tumbles down and breaks her head after hopping upstairs
"to make her bed." Margery Daw "sold her bed and lay upon straw":

> Was she not a dirty slut
> To sell her bed and lie in the dirt. (no. 336)

"Margery Daw" was evidently a synonym for laziness (see no. 335 in
which Jacky "can't work any faster"). "Little Jumping Joan" is also a
term for prostitute; the rhyme about her at first appears one of those
self-evident propositions that the English seem to love in the
rhymes:

> Here am I,
> Little Jumping Joan;
> When nobody's with me
> I'm all alone. (no. 284)

But considering the evidence for her profession, the rhyme also suggests she can't get any business. Another version depicts her attempting to drum up trade:

> Joan, Joan, for your part,
> you love kissing with all your Heart,
> I marry do I, says jumping Joan;
> and therefore to thee I make my moan. (Opie, 251–53)

According to the Opies, Elsie Marley was also an alewife and part-
time prostitute; they quote a long series of verses about her, and
indicate that historical evidence shows that she was a happy and
popular woman, "one of the best documented of the nursery rhyme
characters" (Opie, 160). However, the only verse that is well known
about her ridicules her vanity and laziness:

> Elsie Marley is grown so fine,
> She won't get up to feed the swine,

But lies in bed till eight or nine.
Lazy Elsie Marley. (no. 152)

Macfarlane notes that in part of the period he studied, from 1500 to 1840, adultery and prostitution were regarded with considerable ambivalence; there are several reasons for this ambivalence, but he speculates that one was the strictness of the marriage system: "With monogamy and practically no divorce, it may have been implicitly recognized that adultery was a kind of safety valve . . . High prostitution and adultery rates may have been the price the English paid . . . for the rigid marriage code" (Macfarlane, 244). In the rhymes, this ambivalence emerges in rhymes that acknowledge the presence in society of lusty and willing women but ridicule them at the same time.

"There was an old woman" is the opening line of a number of rhymes, and several other rhymes depict specifically *old* women in various activities. Some of them possess mysterious powers, like the old woman with the broom cited earlier. Others are targets of ridicule. The one named Peg has a wooden head and a cork leg; her neighbors drown her (no. 403). The old woman from Dundee sells rotten plums (no. 145), the old woman of Surrey hurries and harries her family (no. 493), another old woman sends a mouse to the miller (no. 543), but still another is deaf only when it suits her:

Old woman, old woman, shall we go a-shearing?
Speak a little louder, sir, I'm very thick of hearing.
Old woman, old woman, shall I love you dearly?
Thank you very kindly, sir, now I hear you clearly. (no. 536)

The names of the old women are sometimes deliberately ludicrous as well: Slipper-Slopper, Niddity-Nod, Shuttle.

The old woman who made her own way was, in English society between 1500 and 1800, a problem. She "contradicted the patriarchal theory; the ungoverned woman was a threat to the social order" (Todd, 55). The widow was even more ambiguous. If she carried on her own business and managed to support herself, she was proof that a man was not necessary to her livelihood; if she remarried, she signified men's mortality: "The remarriage of any widow confronted every man with the threatening prospect of his own death and the entry of another into his place. The comic widows of the stage personify these contradictory feelings" (Todd, 55). Many of the old women in the rhymes resemble those stage widows: figures of fun because they do not fit neatly into any category and because, underneath, they are threatening to men. In fact, after 1570, more Englishmen inserted a remarriage penalty into their wills, precisely at the time when widows gained more legal power: "This is one more way in which the sense of individualism and the desire to perpetuate family and wealth into the next generation negatively affected women's situation" (Todd, 74).[4] Although the old women in the rhymes are not specifically identified as widows, a number of them are engaged in some kind of business—keeping an alehouse or boarding house, selling eggs or other food—and they tend to look foolish as they carry out these duties: Mrs. Bond, who flies down to the duck pond "in a rage / With plenty of onions and plenty of sage," so her customers can be fed (no. 62); the little woman on her way to market who falls asleep beside the road and has her petticoats cut up by a mischievous pedlar (no. 535); the old woman from Dundee who sells rotten plums (no. 145). But underlying the ostensible economic threat was the threat of the phallic woman, with her mysterious powers only transformed, not abated, in old age: "What are old women made of? / Bushes and thorns and old cow's horns; That's what old women are made of" (B-G, no. 320).

The categorization of women partakes of the ancient power of naming. The stages of women's lives have long been marked with labels—virgin, wife, mother, widow—by both men and women. The Talmud speaks from the father's point of view:

> It is written. A daughter is a vain treasure to her father. From anxiety about her he does not sleep at night; during her early years lest she is seduced, in her adolescence lest she go astray, in her marriageable years lest she does not find a husband, when she is married lest she be childless, and when she is old lest she practice witchcraft. (Quoted in Ellmann, 11)

Women's diaries from the Stuart era show that women themselves divided their lives into three distinct stages: virginity, marriage, and widowhood. Sara Heller Mendelson, who edited these diaries, notes that women were very self-conscious about passing through these stages (191). She also found that these sharply defined life stages of women were balanced by sharply defined class and occupational concerns of men (199) but speculates that had diaries existed for the lower ranks of society, this configuration might be different. However, nursery rhymes form a kind of "diary" of these lower ranks, and suggest that these categories held. Their persistence into the present is suggested by the responses to Geoffrey Gorer's study of English character; asked what wives and husbands wanted from each other, both men and women preserved the dichotomy between work and public life for men and home and privacy for women. Several men further expressed with "epigrammatic neatness" what they wanted in a wife: "Good cook in kitchen. Little lady in Parlour. Mistress in bedroom." And one defined a poor wife thus: "A whore in the kitchen; a cook in bed" (Gorer, 133).

The rhymes about courtship continue to suggest the phallic woman who needs patriarchal control, but the control here takes the form of overvaluation: since husbands are scarce, they require a large expenditure of time and effort on the part of a woman to acquire one; since wives are also scarce, obtaining one requires a large expenditure of time and goods on the part of a man to acquire one. Thus courtship in the rhymes tends to be more mercantile than romantic.

A central feature of English courtship, Macfarlane finds, is the giving and receiving of gifts: rings, gloves, and love letters were among the most common, but the rhymes mention extravagant gifts such as those given "On the first day of Christmas" and after (100) as well as more homely things such as the famous "paper of pins" in the old song. In the rhymes, promises are given more freely and extravagantly than the gifts themselves, as in what is probably the most famous courtship rhyme of all:

> Curly locks, Curly locks,
>   Wilt thou be mine?
> Thou shalt not wash dishes
>   Nor yet feed the swine,
> But sit on a cushion
>   And sew a fine seam,
> And feed upon strawberries,
>   Sugar and cream. (no. 122)

Though such giving may seem quite romantic, it has firmly mercantile underpinnings. Marriage is a contract, an arrangement, a joint venture, an enterprise (all terms which were used for it in England) taking place between two trading partners; such gift giving and promising were the emblems of the enterprise, tokens of good faith that a fair exchange would take place. Many courtship rhymes depict the passionate, extravagant male, offering his all to a shrewd, practical female who knows how to bargain:

> Oh, madam, I will give you the keys of Canterbury. . . .
> Oh, madam, I will give you a fine carved comb. . . .
> Oh, madam, I will give you a pair of shoes of cork. . . .
> Oh, madam, I will give you a sweet silver bell. . . .
> If you will but walk abroad with me,
> If you will but talk with me.

> [The lady refuses all of these in turn, then says:]

> Oh, sir, I will accept the keys to your chest,
> To count your gold and silver when you have gone to rest,
> And I will walk abroad with thee,
> And I will talk with thee! (B-G, no. 286)

One of the incentives for a woman to marry was, and probably is, the control of her husband's wealth upon his death; the lady in this rhyme asks no more than her due, but compared to the man's generous promises, she appears rather heartless. A more famous courtship is that of the little man and little maid (no. 326): he woos her by simply saying, "Will you?" but her response is hardheaded: "You must say a little more and produce a little ore, Ere I to the church will be led." The little man appeals to the "little God of Love," only to encounter:

> Will the flames that you're so rich in
> Make a fire in the kitchen,
> And the little God of Love turn the spit, spit, spit?

> Then the little man he sighed,
> And some say a little cried,
> And his little heart was big with sorrow, sorrow, sorrow;
> I'll be your little slave,
> And if the little that I have,
> Be too little, little dear, I will borrow, borrow, borrow.

> Then the little man so gent,
> Made the little maid relent,
> And set her little soul a thinking, king, king;
> Though his little was but small,
> Yet she had his little all,
> And could have of a cat but her skin, skin, skin. (no. 326)

As noted in the milkmaid rhymes, sexual activity before or outside marriage was, if not condoned, at least acknowledged. Indeed, the imputations of sexual activity to unmarried lovers in the rhymes seem much more widespread than any notions of self-control. The young girl who "fastened her door with a skewer" because she was afraid her lover would come to her (no. 314) is notable because she is an exception. Macfarlane points out that a certain amount of ambivalence about premarital intercourse marked the courtship system in England from 1500 to 1840, partly because the Church officially frowned upon it and yet at the same time stressed the importance of the sexual relationship within a marriage. Thus much of the physical side of courtship was "an attempt to discover the undiscoverable, to gauge the apple by nibbling at the skin. Kissing and fondling hence developed into important and elaborate acts which are not universal in human societies" (Macfarlane, 304). But these too were not merely passionate and emotional exchanges; they were, as Macfarlane's apple metaphor indicates, a mercantile exchange as well, both parties testing the goods to see that a fair exchange was being made. Macfarlane attests to the continuity of these attitudes over the centuries he studied, the late Middle Ages to the nineteenth century (307–308); and Geoffrey Gorer's study of the England of the late 1940s and early 1950s further proves the tenacity of these customs and attitudes. The tacit joining of the natural with the mercantile in the common mind has probably never been as succinctly expressed as by one of Gorer's respondents, a thirty-six-year-old man, to the question, "Do you think a young man should have some sexual experience before he gets married?": "It is only natural," he said, "whenever anything Bird, Beast, or man decide to become mates they have to have that experience, i.e. you would hardly buy anything without taking a look at it first" (Gorer, 111). That women shared this attitude is indicated by the dark-haired "bouncing girl" in the rhymes who knew she would get a husband one way or another: "Twenty pounds will marry me; If twenty won't, then forty shall" (no. 54).

There is a darker side to this exchange system, however, that suggests the archaic fear of women. Two of the most famous courtship rhymes depict a woman making what may not be a fair bargain. "Can you make me a cambric shirt?" (no. 86) depicts the man asking what seems to be an impossible task: making a cambric shirt without seam, washing it in a dry well, and drying it on a bare tree. But the girl responds with even more impossible tasks: find an acre of land between the sea and the land, plow it with a ram's horn, sow it with one peppercorn, reap it with a leather sickle, and bind it with a peacock's feather.

> When you have done and finished your work,
>   Parsley, sage, rosemary, and thyme,
> Then come to me for your cambric shirt,
>   And you shall be a true lover of mine. (no. 86)

The Opies point out that this riddling courtship rhyme has very ancient roots; it certainly suggests the kind of magical tasks that are a feature more of fairy tales than nursery rhymes. Dundes (1980) mentions the use of riddles in betrothal customs as a way of testing male potency; the implication is that courtship and marriage involve doing the impossible, yoking the completely disparate (24–28). Though the Opies do not mention it, the answer to these riddles may be sexual union, the seamless shirt and the acre of land representing the female genitals and the ram's horn and the peppercorn the male genitals and seed. The girl is thus testing the man's potency before she will agree to wed, and the size of the task, as she sets it, is daunting.

A different sort of bargaining informs the famous little rhyme, "Where have you been all the day, My boy Billy?" In this dialogue, Billy has been courting a lady gay, though "she is a young thing, And just come from her mammy." Billy asserts that she is completely fit to be his love and his wife, "As my blade is for my knife," and repeats that she is very young. But when his questioner asks how old she is, Billy answers:

> Twice six, twice seven,
> Twice twenty and eleven,
> Although she is a young thing,
> And just come from her mammy. (no. 45)

The joke is evidently on Billy, who is being offered a woman much older than her living with her "mammy" suggests; he may be the foolish but innocent victim of a bad bargain in this exchange.

Thus the economic concerns of courtship, with their emphasis on making a good bargain, are intricately bound up with the sexual concerns. The fear in these and many other rhymes of the phallic woman is a unconscious component in those concerns, all the more powerful for being unconscious. Throughout these courtship rhymes the picture seems to be that of the ardent, all-giving man being victimized by a scheming woman; the woman tricks the man into a bad bargain, never the other way round. Macfarlane cites a popular seventeenth-century manual, which offered a method for calculating the honesty or dishonesty of a wife; and in 1603 a preacher gave his opinion that "women are like a [tub] full of snakes amongst which there is one eel, and a thousand to one if a man happen upon the eel; and if he get it with his hand, all he has gotten is a wet eel by the tail" (quoted in Macfarlane, 167).

Two rhymes depict the girls doing the courting: while the girls' ardor might make them appear to be exceptions to the pattern of eager male and calculating woman, neither of these girls has much dignity:

> When shall we be married,
>   Billy, my pretty lad?
> We'll be married tomorrow,
>   If you think it good.
> Shall we be married no sooner,
>   Billy, my pretty lad?
> Would you be married tonight?
>   I think the girl is mad. (no. 43).

The earliest version of this, a Scottish song, changes the last line of each stanza to "I think the auld runt be gane mad" (Opie, 74). In neither version does the female come off very well. Nor does the woman who wooed a swine:

> There was a lady loved a swine,
>   Honey, quoth she,
> Pig-hog wilt thou be mine?
>   Hoogh, quoth he.
>
> I'll build thee a silver sty,
>   Honey, quoth she,
> And in it thou shalt lie.
>   Hoogh, quoth he.
>
> Pinned with a silver pin,
>   Honey, quoth she,
> That thou may go out and in.
>   Hoogh, quoth he.

Wilt thou have me now,
    Honey, quoth she.
Speak or my heart will break.
    Hoogh, quoth he. (no. 294)

Read against "Curly Locks" or "There was a little man," this rhyme
becomes a satiric inversion of the classic situation; instead of the
ardent male offering gifts to a disdainful female, we see an ardent
female offering gifts not to a man but to a hog. Walter Crane's illustration for this rhyme literalizes not only this inversion but the
proverb about casting one's pearls before swine. Crane juxtaposed a
lovely woman in a Grecian gown and setting, with a large, tusked,
muscular hog overturning a trough from which spill pearls (Figure
5). Despite the dignity Crane's Greek motif lends, such a woman can
only appear a complete fool. Thus in almost every courtship situation in the rhymes, the woman is the object of fear or scorn: she is
either phallic or castrated, greedily powerful or passive, scheming or
foolish.

Macfarlane marshals several pages of quotations from literature
attesting to the importance of romantic love in English culture from
the early Middle Ages through the midnineteenth century. He concludes that, since his sources are mostly from poetry and drama,
they may reflect an upper-class minority: "It is very difficult through
poetry to penetrate to the lower levels," he says, though he suggests
that many popular ballads were equally "love-soaked" and reflected
the same passions (189). Had he looked at the nursery rhymes, he
might indeed have "penetrated to the lower levels," and there he
would have found certainly a concern with courtship, and even a
touch of what he calls a "strange, overwhelming passion which
could strike anyone and which could lead to delight or disaster"
(190). But he would have found an almost complete absence of the
reciprocal romantic love we associated with courting. Instead, the
rhymes show not so much love-soaked courtship as defensive men
and women overvaluing each other in response to archaic, unconscious fears.

Among "Mother Goose's Wise Sayings," the Baring-Goulds
place this famous ditty, which generally sums up the attitudes toward marriage—for both men and women—that permeate the
rhymes:

Figure 5. Illustration by Walter Crane from *The Baby's Opera.* de Grummond Children's Literature Research Collection.

Scissors and string, scissors and string,
When a man's single he lives like a king.
Needles and pins, needles and pins,
When a man marries, his trouble begins. (B-G no. 766)

Unlike the fairy tales, where marriage is generally the conclusion of the story and thus never explored in detail, becoming only an emblem of fullness or completeness, the rhymes often show marriage as an angry and aggressive relationship in which neither gender is displayed sympathetically. The overvaluation of courtship becomes the devaluation of a relationship that may have been a bad bargain.

Macfarlane begins his study of marriage in England with some quotations from Charles Darwin as Darwin tried to decide whether to marry or to remain single. In 1838, Darwin set down in detail reasons for both decisions, and his ruminations survive on a scrap of paper. Among the reasons to avoid marriage are loss of freedom, income, and time: "Perhaps my wife won't like London, then the sentence is banishment and degradation with indolent, idle fool." The chief reason to marry is companionship: "Imagine living all one's days solitarily in smoky dirty London House—Only picture to yourself a nice soft wife on a sofa with good fire, and books and music perhaps—" (quoted in Macfarlane, 3–4). Companionship won the day, and Darwin did indeed marry. But his exercise in decision making exemplifies attitudes toward marriage that have been a peculiar feature of English culture since the Middle Ages. Macfarlane calls English marriage the "Malthusian marriage system": its chief features are delayed marriage, individual decision, and economic alternatives to children, and one of its results is the control of population. Unlike most other societies the world over, in which marriage is a group activity rendering social and economic reproduction identical and each new child an asset, English culture stresses the individual nature of the decision; there are plenty of alternatives to marriage and to children, and the companionship of marriage needs to be weighed against them. As with Darwin, though, it is evidently a powerful incentive to wed.

This Western notion of "companionate" marriage, which Macfarlane finds unusual, resulted in some emphasis on equality in marriage. Aphra Behn and others stressed the importance of balance and due proportion (Macfarlane, 161), a concern which finds its way into one of the most famous marriage rhymes of all:

Jack Sprat could eat no fat,
     His wife could eat no lean,
And so between them both, you see,
     They licked the platter clean. (no. 264)

But far more common is the attitude in such rhymes as:

Tommy Trot, a man of law,
Sold his bed and lay upon straw;
Sold the straw and slept on grass,
To buy his wife a looking-glass. (no. 518)

The inevitable results of marriage are those that afflict Jemmy Dawson, in a rhyme that echoes an old jump-rope rhyme:

First he bought a porridge-pot,
     Then he bought a ladle;
Then he got a wife and child,
     And then he bought a cradle. (no. 270)

Many marriage rhymes express a mercantile attitude; "buying" a wife is mentioned occasionally, and often implied. In such situations, companionship and equality seem to matter less than housekeeping skills:

When I was a little boy I lived by myself,
And all the bread and cheese I got I laid upon a shelf,
The rats and the mice they made such a strife,
I had to go to London to buy me a wife.

The streets were so broad and the lanes were so narrow,
I was forced to bring my wife home in a wheelbarrow.
The wheelbarrow broke and my wife had a fall,
Farewell wheelbarrow, little wife and all. (no. 71)

The sequel to this adventure appears in a Scots version, which complains that the wife was crippled and refused to eat bacon or beef, "For fyling o' her teeth" (Opie, 96). Housekeeping skills are also important in this rhyme:

I married a wife by the light of the moon,
     A tidy housewife, a tidy one;
She never gets up until it is noon,
     And I hope she'll prove a tidy one.

And when she gets up she is slovenly laced,
     A tidy housewife, a tidy one;

She takes up the poker to roll out the paste,
　　And I hope she'll prove a tidy one.

She churns her butter in a boot,
　　A tidy housewife, a tidy one;
And instead of a churnstaff she puts in her foot,
　　And I hope she'll prove a tidy one.

She lays her cheese on the scullery shelf,
　　A tidy housewife, a tidy one;
And she never turns it till it turns itself,
　　And I hope she'll prove a tidy one. (B-G, no. 288)

The ironic humor of this rhyme suggests, as did others cited earlier, that the husband has been taken in by a woman who did not bargain honestly.

Two very famous rhymes suggest relationships between women and men based on ridicule, a form of aggression in which we denigrate what we can't understand or control. This connection makes a famous nonsense rhyme less nonsensical:

Hey diddle diddle,
The cat and the fiddle,
The cow jumped over the moon;
The little dog laughed
To see such sport,
And the dish ran away with the spoon. (no. 213)

Cat, cow, and moon are all archetypal feminine symbols, as are kitchen implements like the dish and the spoon. In this rhyme, they are in chaos, while the dog, an invariably male figure throughout the rhymes, laughs at them. Another famous rhyme, which at first seems to suggest some equality between the sexes and their foolishness, is "Jack and Jill" (no. 254). Their journey up the hill seems to symbolize some sort of agreement, and their falling down some mutual sexual activity. But the end of the rhyme depicts Jack going to "Dame Dob" for sympathy, which he doesn't get from Jill:

Then Jill came in,
And she did grin,
To see Jack's paper plaster;
Her mother whipt her,
Across her knee,
For laughing at Jack's disaster.

Here, the female ridicules the male's plight, but then is punished for it. One illustrator shows Jill being spanked across her bare bottom while Jack stands watching. (See Opie, 225.) Although these are not overtly marriage rhymes, when read alongside the large body of other rhymes about men and women, they continue to suggest aggression toward the feared female.

Beating wives is a theme of several rhymes, one of which appears in *Mother Goose's Wise Sayings*: "A woman, a spaniel, and a walnut tree, The more you beat them the better they be" (B-G, no. 767). The most famous battling spouses, Punch and Judy, are stock characters from centuries-old Italian puppet theater; the name *Punch* may come from the Italian for "little chicken" and may refer to the size and shape of Punch's nose, and, by common folk implication, his phallus. But in English *to punch* also means to hit sharply with the fist, and may be related to *puncheon*, a tool for perforating; all of this adds up to sexual violence, the image of which, in the Punch and Judy puppet shows, the English as well as the Italians seem to have found hilarious:

Punch and Judy
  Fought for a pie;
Punch gave Judy
  A knock in the eye.

Says Punch to Judy
  Will you have more?
Says Judy to Punch,
  My eye is sore. (no. 423)

In the puppet shows, Judy is depicted as a shrew, who evidently deserves her punishment, but the humor lies in the beating. An equally long-lived joke, at one time printed under the title of "A New Year's Gift for Shrews," is this famous rhyme:

Tom married a wife on Sunday,
Beat her well on Monday,
Bad was she on Tuesday,
Middling was she on Wednesday,
Worse was she on Thursday,
Dead was she on Friday;
Glad was Tom on Saturday night
To bury his wife on Sunday. (no. 509)

There are several versions of this rhyme, some of which specify that the wife began to scold or that Tom bought a stick to beat her with.

The 1620 "New Years Guift for Shrews" illustrated a precursor of this rhyme with a sequential drawing of the events of each day, ending with the devil chasing the wife down the road with a pitchfork (reproduced as Plate XX in Opie after p. 410). The Baring-Goulds note, without a trace of wonder, that this rhyme was "perhaps devised to teach children the days of the week" (Baring-Gould, 105).

Freud's complex examination of the child-beating fantasy (1919) focused on the mental life of women, and led him to the conclusion that the fantasy had both sadistic and masochistic components, interacting with each other in a complicated sequence. In one of its phases, the second and unconscious one, it represents the consummation of the oedipal attachment to the father: the interpretation is, "I am being beaten (i.e. caressed) by my father." But while Freud tended to assign a large portion of masochism to women, by no means did he perceive it as exclusively feminine; it is a "feminine" trait (Freud was often frustrated by the inadequacy of that term) occurring in both sexes. In both men and women, he believed, it represents the need to be punished by the father; thus in women it is part of the "positive" oedipal situation, while in men it is a regression to preoedipal, "feminine" position vis-à-vis the father: "People who harbor phantasies of this kind develop a special sensitiveness and irritability toward anyone whom they can include in the class of fathers" (Freud 1919, 123). This would explain the evident prevalence, so much a part of English literature, of "la vice Anglaise" among the inhabitants of a boys' public (that is, boarding) school. It would also explain, at least in part, the tenacity and popularity of these rhymes and of the Punch and Judy spectacle. For women, they represent an inverted fulfillment of their oedipal desire for their fathers, along with the feeling of guilt and the imposition of punishment for that same desire. For men, they represent the fulfillment of an even more regressive desire: feminine passivity before their fathers. Moreover, since the women in these rhymes are scolding and shrewish—that is, castrating and phallic—the men and women who enjoy these rhymes can also nourish their archaic fantasies of revenge against their all-powerful mothers. Wife beating may also be an example of behavior once at least partially institutionalized, but now existing as noninstitutionalized. The rhymes suggest that it was once accepted and acceptable; now they suggest that the impulse to beat a spouse still exists and offer a way of fantasizing about it without actually carrying it out. There are many more complexities in the issues raised by these rhymes, but these speculations offer at least a clue to their overdetermination, and reinforce the argument that the rhymes concerning courtship and marriage supply voice and emblem in remarkable numbers to men's and women's preoedipal fantasies.

One of the favorite stock characters in much folklore is the cuckolded husband; Elizabethan Englishmen and women found his plight hilarious, as have many others.[5] The henpecked and meek husband is still a favorite in many popular forms of literature and mass media; Caspar Milquetoast is one name for him, and Walter Mitty, Thurber's creation, is another. It is interesting then to note the almost complete *absence* of such characters in the nursery rhymes. Men are scolded and made fools of, but they generally do not take it quietly. Only Tommy Trot, the man of law who sold everything to buy his wife a looking glass (no. 518), seems to fit this stereotype. There are several references to *small* husbands, however:

> I had a little husband,
> No bigger than my thumb;
> I put him in a pint-pot,
> And there I bid him drum.
> I bought a little horse
> That galloped up and down;
> I bridled him, and saddled him
> And sent him out of town.
> I gave him some garters
> To garter up his hose,
> And a little silk handkerchief
> To wipe his pretty nose. (no. 234)

This mannikin is an analogue to Tom Thumb, a remarkably popular figure in fairy tales and chapbooks. Such male figures may be called "husbands," but they seem more like children, in that the "wives" care for them as they would infants, with kindly and indulgent nurturing. As with the beating fantasy, this one is overdetermined and no doubt has a strong appeal for both sexes. However, instead of fear of the archaic phallic mother, these rhymes express the early love of the nurturing mother, still a giantess but a gentle one, and once again testify to the flexibility of the archetype of the female throughout the rhymes.

One of the most famous rhymes of all depicts a curious relationship between male and female. In its best-known form, "Old Mother Hubbard" consists of an opening verse of six lines:

> Old Mother Hubbard
> Went to the cupboard,
> To fetch her poor dog a bone;
> But when she came there
> The cupboard was bare
> And so the poor dog had none. (no. 365)

This is followed by thirteen verses of four lines each, all describing the same pattern: Mother Hubbard going somewhere for food or clothes for the dog, and finding the dog, upon her return, playing in some way unrelated to her gift:

> She went to the fruiterer's
> To buy him some fruit;
> But when she came back
> He was playing the flute.
>
> She went to the tailor's
> To buy him a coat;
> But when she came back
> He was riding a goat.

The proliferation of these middle verses, and the similarity among them, suggest a keen pleasure in their structure and what they describe: a woman repeatedly going and coming, bringing food and clothing to a creature who remains in one place. Indeed, they seem to describe one of the earliest human memories in our culture: the infant's locomotor helplessness and the contrasting mobility of its mother, her face appearing, disappearing, reappearing to the infant as she cares for its bodily needs—a kind of English folk precursor to the famous *fort-da* game in Freud's *Beyond the Pleasure Principle* (1920). Freud observed that his grandson never cried when his mother left him alone, but that he especially enjoyed playing at making objects "disappear" and then return, saying what his mother interpreted as *fort* (German for "gone") when he hid them, and then what Freud called "a joyful *da*" (meaning "there") when he found them (14–16). Freud believed the pleasure in the game resulted from the boy's taking a situation in which he was passive—the mother's departure—and repeating it as a game, thereby making himself an active participant, just as does Mother Hubbard's dog, and just as do many children who enjoy some version of "peekaboo."

Certainly the popularity of this rhyme suggests that it taps into a complex set of memories and pleasures for a great many people. *The Comic Adventures of Old Mother Hubbard and her Dog* first appeared in print as a toy book published in 1805 by "J. Harris" and supposedly authored by Sarah Catherine Martin. However, the character and the name "Mother Hubbard" were already well known in English folklore (though her association with a dog evidently was not). More interestingly, in 1803 had appeared a publication by "T. Evans" called *Old Dame Trot and her Comical Cat*, which bore several striking resemblances to "Old Mother Hubbard." It described an old woman seeking food for her cat, finding none, visiting a butcher's, and returning to find the cat "dead at her feet." Dame Trot then visits the undertaker's, returning to find the cat alive after all; eleven more verses continue in the same pattern (Opie, 320–21). The Opies note that "Dame Trot" was probably already known in England at least a hundred years prior to its appearance in 1803, but they also point out that the publication of "Old Mother Hubbard" in 1805, derivative though it evidently was, was a phenomenal success, selling "upwards of ten thousand copies" in a few months, and reprinted, pirated, copied, parodied, and expanded by anonymous versifiers many times over until the present. They estimate that a new version of the rhyme has been published each year since 1805 (Opie, 320–21). Such a situation suggests that the popularity of the rhyme lies in something other than its humorous series of rhythmic verses so similar to "Dame Trot."

Three seemingly small changes in the "Dame Trot" verse appear to be crucial. With the shift from "Dame Trot" to "Mother Hubbard," the focus of the rhyme shifted from notions of wifehood to notions of motherhood, encouraging associated unconscious memories in both adults and children who read or heard the rhyme. "Trot" humorously reflects the woman's actions, but the rhyming of "Hubbard" with "cupboard" suggests notions of kitchens, enclosed spaces, food, perhaps even womb and breasts—all richer associations with motherhood than "Dame Trot" encourages. Further, the shift from a "comical cat" to a dog opens the rhyme to more associations with mothers and children in English-speaking culture. Cats are known to us for their independence: they gather their own food, clean themselves, defend themselves from predators, and act as predators themselves early on. Dogs, on the other hand, have for centuries been regarded almost as children in English households— petted, scolded, made to obey, fed from the table, generally encouraged to behave as dependents. Moreover, the dog is identified as male, as opposed to the female cat, creating in the rhyme a neat gender separation that suggests the culturally encouraged separation of the child from the mother as it matures. And much of the dog's play seems decidedly masculine if not actually phallic: he smokes a pipe, rides a goat, plays the flute. Thus in this rhyme, beloved of both boys and girls, phallic sexuality is offered as the norm—as it probably is in most patriarchal cultures.

Old Mother Hubbard herself has not escaped some phallic identity; though in the rhyme she finds no "bone" in the cupboard, suggesting a child's fantasy of the castrated woman, almost all the illustrations of her well into the nineteenth century make her strongly resemble the character Punch, with a very prominent nose, a pointed hat and a long cloak (Figure 6). Such a cloak was called a "Mother Hubbard" during the nineteenth century (Carpenter and Prichard, 365) and still gives its name to certain kinds of voluminous dress.

Though the dog/woman relationship here seems to partake of the "little husband" motif, which shows up in other rhymes, the dog's identification with the home as well as his implied smallness and playfulness suggests more a child than a husband. For adults then, he may replicate the same fantasy as the "little husband" rhymes: the adult become a child again and being indulged by a large but fond and nurturing woman. "Old Mother Hubbard" adds more to the fantasy, however: the woman, for all her efforts, cannot finally anticipate or satisfy the child's needs. The "child" in this case is not overtly demanding, but rather constantly changing, slipping out of the woman's grasp, refusing finally to be possessed by her, even by her love and care. Such a fantasy may be part of every child's psychic heritage, male or female: it involves both the sense that the mother never gave enough love (milk, holding) and the sense that her care would smother, possess, prevent growth and freedom, if the child acquiesced too much. Thus the insatiable demands of the child are its very life, and the space between mother and child essential to its survival.

Figure 6. Old Mother Hubbard. Anonymous illustration. Special Collections, Milbank Memorial Library, Teachers College, Columbia University.

The famous last stanza emphasizes this space, but in such a way that both must acknowledge a kind of defeat as well as their separate worlds:

> The dame made a curtsy,
>   The dog made a bow;
> The dame said, Your servant,
>   The dog said, Bow-wow.

At the moment when equality and communication seem the most likely, language steps in to separate them once again. The dame looks foolish in her obsequious attempts to communicate with a dog, and the dog's many accomplishments pale with the recognition that he has not mastered the language. This too is part of the infantile fantasy that lies at the heart of this rhyme: the child's knowledge that language is finally power, and that it does not yet have this power.

"Old Mother Hubbard," then, speaks to the relationship between the sexes at the deepest level: the preoedipal, the infantile, when the child's relationship to its mother is at its closest and most ambivalent. That it should speak to this concern as well as to the concern with language in such controlled, sophisticated language itself—balanced, musical, orderly, humorous—is further testament to its wisdom. This rhyme is one of the most richly overdetermined of them all; its enduring popularity is not surprising.

Mary Ellmann's 1968 feminist classic *Thinking About Women* argues powerfully, and with frequently sardonic humor, that stereotypes of women pervade most thinking about them and that both men and women tend to think "by sexual analogy." Some of the stereotypical qualities that attach themselves to women are formlessness, passivity, instability, confinement, irrationality, and compliancy, all of which appear in the rhymes, as well as what Ellmann calls the "two incorrigible figures," the witch and the shrew. The point is, finally, that most thinking about women, both men's as well as women's own thinking, is predicated on fantasy. And Jacques Lacan has tried to demonstrate that the phallus is itself a fantasy, a creation of the imagination to compensate for what is actually an absence or lack. (See especially the essays in Lacan 1985.) All of these nursery rhymes about men and women, and their relationship through courtship and marriage, have certainly revealed such fantasy-governed thinking, by and about both men and women.

Kleinian psychoanalysis suggests that fantasy originates in earliest childhood, as the infant copes with its dependence on a seemingly all-powerful female, who can both give and withhold life itself. The fantasy projections in the rhymes of the phallic woman are partly relics of this early conflict. But their persistence through the rhymes and through many other cultural products suggests that these projections serve also to mitigate ongoing conflicts in the relationship between the sexes, and help maintain society itself in its task of channeling fears and aggressions into useful energy. Anna Freud pointed out that such projections allow us to "form valuable positive attachments and so to consolidate our relations with one another": such is the "human ego's great capacity for transformation" (123, 141). The id with its basic drives remains relatively immutable; the ego, however, finds myriad ways to cope. These rhymes testify to the ego's resilience, and to the resulting resilience of the culture in providing spheres such as courtship and marriage where human beings may both express and contain their powerful feelings and fantasies.

Pat-a-cake, pat-a-cake, baker's man,
Bake me a cake as fast as you can;
Pat it and prick it, and mark it with B,
Put it in the oven for baby and me.

CHAPTER 4 **Baby and Me**

The Complementary

Uses of Holding

and Playing

The group of rhymes to be examined in this chapter, a much smaller group than those in previous chapters, consists of rhymes that most directly encourage touching: lullabies, and what the Opies call "infant amusements"—rhymes for bouncing, tickling, clapping, and other kinds of touching that are less than soothing. Indeed, these rhymes demonstrate the curious contrast in the way adults in English-speaking culture handle an infant's body. They alternate between holding it closely, encouraging its growing sense of its own wholeness, and then, in the name of play, threatening it with disintegration by pretending to drop it or to split it into pieces. Such activities, accompanied by feeding and by the blandishments of language represent some of the infant's earliest experience with another person, with the external world in which it must define itself.

The work of Melanie Klein and her school has focused on the aggressive instincts of the infant. Unable to possess its mother's breast whenever it wants, Kleinians theorize, it reacts with rage and hostility, fantasizing methods of retaliation against the "bad" breast. This early complex of feelings Klein termed the "paranoid-schizoid position," a term that emphasizes the persecutory nature of the fantasy, the splitting mechanism that is the infant's defense, and the structural element in the notion: it is a position, not a phase, and thus it may be returned to again and again. When the infant begins to perceive the mother as a person, not a split-off breast, it regrets its rage and its fantasied destruction of the breast, and attempts to make "reparation," to repair the damaged object (mother/breast) that exists in its fantasy. Klein called this the "depressive position," and its existence forms the core of her theory of normal development: the infant must pass through this position in order to perceive the external world with its objects, *and* its internal world with its objects, in a healthy relation to itself. The depressive position too is more structural than chronological; it too can—indeed must—be returned to time and again, as objects within and without blend into a concept of reality. Both positions are crucial to the infant's evolving sense of self.[1]

The lullabies and amusements act as a response, or even a kind of mirror, to these Kleinian positions. The holding that usually accompanies the lullaby offers reassurance to the infant's fantasies of destruction and disintegration, whereas the words occasionally sing of just such destruction. The striking, pinching, jouncing, and dropping that accompany the amusements threaten the realization of the infant's fears and fantasies; yet they are most often performed with smiles and laughter and generally end with some kind of holding or restoration. In a sense, these rhymes stand in a mirror relationship to each other; the lullabies' words often threaten while their actions soothe; the violent actions accompanying the amusements frighten while the rhythm and repetition of their words offer reassurance.

These rhymes, and those in the following chapter, differ from most of the rhymes discussed previously in an important way. They were composed and intended for children; they are conscious attempts to communicate with a child, and as such, they consciously or unconsciously address the child's most basic fears and concerns. These concerns have been variously identified. Winnicott enumerated going to pieces, falling forever, having no relationship to the body, having no orientation, and complete isolation as the "unthinkable anxieties" for a child's developing ego (1965, 58). Margaret Mahler listed three "paramount anxiety-generating conditions of childhood": fear of object loss coupled with the fear of losing the object's love; awareness of bodily pressures; and reaction to anatomical difference between the sexes (Mahler, 229). Mahler further points out that these conditions converge during what she calls the "rapprochement period," a period usually during the second year of life, from fourteen to twenty-four months, during which the child's perception of itself as a separate being emerges (228–29 and 291–92).[2] Interestingly, this is also the period when experience tells us that nursery rhymes offer the most pleasure to children.

Winnicott expressed the main task of the emerging self thus: "The question is: how to be isolated without having to be insulated?" (1965, 187). These rhymes acknowledge the "isolation" of the body as the infant gains control over all its parts, but in their shared pleasures of touch and language, the rhymes help children understand that selfhood need not be synonymous with insulation. And this is true for the adults who share these rhymes with their children. Though the great majority of adults have achieved selfhood, they remember unconsciously the fears that accompanied this achievement. Like the animal rhymes and the rhymes about the sexes, these rhymes allow the expression of those "unthinkable anxieties" while encouraging and complementing their mastery.

The lullaby is one of the oldest poetic forms, sometimes even called the "genesis of all song" (Opie, 18); its folk tradition reaches back to Roman times and its literary tradition is long and honorable. However, most known lullabies are probably not older than the sixteenth or seventeenth century. The meanings of the words most associated with them—*lull* and *bye*—are somewhat shadowy, "lull" evidently from the echoic root "la" and related to *loll*, whereas "bye" is a word used (with *hush* and *rock* as well as *lull*) to send the infant to sleep. The earliest appearance of "lulla" as a "quiescence word in cradle songs" seems to have been in 1315 (Opie, 19). The lullabies collected by the Opies and the Baring-Goulds occupy a small space in both collections: the Opies print only nine, and the Baring-Goulds five more besides the nine they reprint from the Opie collection. Yet one of them is probably the most widely known and frequently sung rhyme in the entire collection.

One of the less surprising motifs in these rhymes is that of the parents as royalty. This fantasy, evidently a common one in children's conscious and unconscious thoughts, is here offered as comfort to the child:

Rock-a-bye, baby,
  Thy cradle is green,
Father's a nobleman,
  Mother's a queen. (no. 23)

Hush-a-bye, baby,
  Daddy is near,
Mammy's a lady,
  And that's very clear. (no. 21)

The likelihood that such rhymes were at times sung by nurses suggests the wish-fulfilling fantasies of a serving girl as well.

Another unsurprising motif is the absent father, but it takes an unexpected form. The tenderest version is this famous song, and its many variations:

Bye, baby bunting,
Daddy's gone a-hunting,
Gone to get a rabbit skin
To wrap baby bunting in. (no. 25)

In one rhyme, papa will come home in a gig (B-G, no. 559); in another, the baby will have an apple, a plum, and a "rattle-basket" when dad comes home (B-G, no. 563). The famous song "Hush, little baby, don't say a word" (B-G, no. 558) is a list of all the things "papa will buy you": a mockingbird, a looking glass, a diamond ring, a billy goat, etc. Through such rhymes, English-speaking children learn early to depend on father for the things money will buy.

The number of references to money and to buying things is noteworthy in such a small group of rhymes, especially in lullabies, where we might assume that the infant can have no knowledge of the things described. This may partly result from the actual poverty of the composers of these rhymes and represent their unfulfilled wishes; on another level, they hint at the anal motifs that underlie these rhymes. The association of money and feces, which Freud delineated in 1908, was acknowledged long before Freud in many folk sayings and myths. Freud theorized that it results from the sublimation of anal erotism—that is, the erotic interest in defecation noticeable in young children and probably present as well in infants; as this interest is extinguished, the knowledge of and interest in money emerges to take its place (Freud 1963 [1908], 32). This is one way the anal phase in children remains present in adults. This motif in the lullabies, while certainly reflecting a conscious desire to placate and provide for one's child, may also reflect this unconscious anality, repressed from the adult's childhood.[3]

Freud also pointed out the sadism associated with the anal phase; in his view, this second pregenital phase corresponded with the appearance of aggressive tendencies. Such tendencies partly result from the child's reluctance to submit to toilet training, to give up his anal erotism and carry out his first "'repression' of his possibilities for pleasure" (Freud 1962 [1905], n. 53).[4] Such aggressions seem to be encouraged in this lullaby:

> Hush-a-bye a baa-lamb,
> Hush-a-bye a milk cow,
> You shall have a little stick
> To beat the naughty bow-wow. (no. 13)

The sadism of the mother or nurse is blatant in this lullaby:

> Baby, baby, naughty baby,
> Hush, you squalling thing, I say.
> Peace this moment, peace, or maybe
> Bonaparte will pass this way.
>
> Baby, baby, he's a giant,
> Tall and black as Rouen steeple,
> And he breakfasts, dines, rely on't.
> Every day on naughty people.
>
> Baby, baby, if he hears you,
> As he gallops past the house,
> Limb from limb at once he'll tear you,
> Just as pussy tears a mouse.
>
> And he'll beat you, beat you, beat you,
> And he'll beat you all to pap,
> And he'll eat you, eat you, eat you,
> Every morsel snap, snap, snap. (no. 16)

The Opies comment that other names besides Bonaparte's have been substituted over the years in this request for "peace by intimidation" (Opie, 59). Certainly its overt anger and frustration suggest long-standing hostility suddenly released, and although the threat of devouring is here displaced onto Bonaparte, the rhyme implies that it is really the speaker who would like to devour the baby. Such a greedy and hostile impulse is one of the most archaic in the human psyche, and as we know, fairy and folk tales as well as nursery rhymes are replete with such devouring as well as with other aggressions and threats.

Nicholas Tucker points out, in his brief essay on the lullabies, that such threats brought "vicarious relief to the mother" (21). He quotes a Spanish lullaby in which the mother tells the baby, "Go away! You are not my child, your mother was a gypsy," and notes that since the point of the song was to lull the baby back to sleep, the hands and voice of the mother must belie her words. Tucker believes that lullabies that make extravagant promises to the infant also have an element of aggression; they are "equivalent to the traditional verbal tricks that adults have always inflicted on children, whereby hopes are first raised and then dashed again" (25).

Such threatening lullabies are balanced to a degree by gentler ones, but where the overt threat recedes, the element of complaint emerges, an element that can also threaten the loss of parental love, the loss of the parents themselves, or even the loss of the infant's life. Tucker cites an Italian lullaby which complains, "Thou has robbed me of my heart and of all feeling" (21), and the Baring-Goulds offer one which has a gentle and loving first verse, but then complains,

> Care is heavy, therefore sleep you;
> You are care, and care must keep you. (B-G, no. 557)

Another lullaby is unusual in that it is sung by a father, and that it retains the old pronunciation of *baby* (Opie, 19):

> Hush thee, my babby,
> Lie still with they daddy,
> Thy mammy has gone to the mill,
> To grind thee some wheat,
> To make thee some meat,
> Oh, my dear babby, lie still. (no. 14)

The weariness in the last line must be familiar to every parent. But probably the most poignant of such complaining lullabies is this one:

> Bye, O my baby,
> When I was a lady,
> O then my baby didn't cry;

But my baby is weeping
For want of good keeping,
O I fear my poor baby will die. (no. 17)

Such a direct mention of the possibility of death may seem out of place in a lullaby, until we remember the most ubiquitous bedtime prayer taught to English-speaking children: "Now I lay me down to sleep; I pray the Lord my soul to keep. If I should die before I wake, I pray the Lord my soul to take" (no. 245). And the most famous lullaby of all, gently sung by countless mothers over the centuries, threatens disaster:

Hush-a-bye, baby, on the tree top,
When the wind blows, the cradle will rock;
When the bough breaks the cradle will fall,
Down will come baby, cradle, and all. (no. 22)

Cradles may have been rocked by the wind from time to time (see Opie, 61–62), but such historical information cannot explain the tenacious popularity of the rhyme. It may result from the rhyme's acknowledgement of one of the most basic human anxieties: the inevitability of falling. Many rhymes involve some kind of falling, and its complex symbolism is discussed later in this chapter. This rhyme differs from others, however, because it is a lullaby, not an accompaniment to a game for older children. Modern illustrators tend to hint at insecurity instead of actual falling, usually depicting a baby tucked tightly in an upright cradle even though the cradle may be suspended from a tree limb. An early illustrator, however, confronted the rhyme more directly—"the cradle *will* fall"—and drew a baby in a cradle really falling from a tree (Figure 7).

Such an emotionally charged image is not one we expect or desire today, for it calls up especially intense associations: infancy, falling asleep, and the mother, a connection which also interested the English poet Samuel Taylor Coleridge. In her study of his notebooks, Margery Durham (1985) finds falling associated in Coleridge's mind with the loss of the maternal touch, a loss which causes "fear, guilt, and finally death" (Durham, 177). Coleridge jotted:

Sense of diminished Contact explains the falling asleep—/this *is* Fear . . . . To fall asleep—is not a event in the body well represented by this phrase—is it in *excess*, when on first *dropping* asleep we *fall* down precipices, or *sink* down, all things *sinking* beneath us, or *drop down*. (Quoted in Durham, 177)

The Complementary Uses of Holding and Playing   81

Figure 7. Hush a bye baby. Anonymous illustration from *The Only True Mother Goose Melodies*. The Central Children's Room, Donnell Library Center, The New York Public Library.

Hush-a-bye, baby" acknowledges such a fear of falling, this loss, and the guilt and the notions of death that accompany it. In the mother who sings it resides the archaic memory of her own such falling, of the loss of her mother's touch. Singing it to her own child may be a form of therapy for her, and the beginning of her inevitable separation from the child.

Mary Ellmann has commented on the hostility of a mother toward her child and the sense in our culture that this attitude should not be acknowledged, noting that patriarchal language tends to identify motherhood with creativity, while most women regard it as "having done no more than indulge the body in a prolonged vagary of its own design" (Ellmann, 64). Adrienne Rich is more polemical about the "sacred calling" that is motherhood in our culture, pointing out that the beginning of the idealization of motherhood was commensurate with the emergence of women from the home. Mothers were not allowed to have any negative feelings about their duties; Rich quotes from a nineteenth-century best-seller by John S. C. Abbott, *The Mother at Home*:

> She must learn to control herself, to subdue her own passions; she must set her children an example of meekness and of equanimity . . . Let a mother feel grieved, and manifest her grief when her child does wrong; let her, with calmness and reflection, use the discipline which the case requires; but never let her manifest irritated feeling, or give utterance to an angry expression. (Quoted in Rich, 45)

This feminine image (the angelic Marmee in *Little Women* is a classic example in popular literature) constitutes, Rich notes, a "dangerous archetype" for both sexes, encouraging the unrealistic separation of love and forgiveness from the masculine values of competition and contempt for weakness (Rich, 52).

Freud found that the dominant feature of the sadistic-anal organization of the instincts is its ambivalence. Aims of activity—that is, mastery—conflict with aims of passivity—allowing events to take place. These "opposing pairs of instincts are developed to an approximately equal extent": this is genuine ambivalence (Freud 1962 [1905], 64). Such ambivalence informs most women's attitudes toward pregnancy and to their children. Adrienne Rich puts it most eloquently: "the murderous alternation between bitter resentment and raw-edged nerves, and blissful gratification and tenderness . . . I *love them*. But it's in the enormity and inevitability of this love that the sufferings lie" (Rich, 21–22).

The ambivalence in the mother singing such a lullaby provides not only therapy for her, but may begin in her child the essential process of separation. Speculation on how and when a child might understand the ambivalence in the words may be impossible to document, but the understanding of the mother's affect may come relatively early. A study which showed that mothers' caretaking regimes were influenced by their unconscious attitudes toward their children (Hartmann, Kris, and Loewenstein, 111) suggests that very young children might feel the effects of ambivalence. Along with other elements in the environment, the mother's ambivalence may begin to move the infant beyond the mirror stage, when the mother/infant relationship appears to other observers most balanced and secure. It suggests to the infant that the mother has other interests, and that it must inevitably separate from her. Though this realization may be distressing, the formation of the child's sense of self requires it.

Most of the lullabies discussed here are seldom used today, with the notable exception of the most ambivalent of all—the lullaby that embeds an image of falling and disaster in the gentlest and most natural sounds and movement (rocking, the wind in the trees). The persistence of this lullaby attests to the tenacity of anger as it emerges through a tightly controlled poetic form gently sung to an infant; in Nicholas Tucker's words, this lullaby is an exercise in controlled hatred (20–21), and as such, it represents in remarkably small space the deepest and most troubling ambivalence. The Baring-Goulds cite James O. Halliwell as saying that of all the rhymes, the lullabies "come the closest to being true poetry" (Baring-Gould, 223). They do not explore the implications of this statement, but Halliwell, and probably the Baring-Goulds, may be responding to this deep ambivalence in them. As it is embedded in the gentlest words and offered in the gentlest situations, it represents an achievement for language.

Rhymes that accompany infant amusements are probably among the oldest verses extant; an example from Rome in A.D. 50 has its equivalent in modern-day New York, and a version of "Handy-Dandy" (in which an object is juggled from one hand to another) was mentioned in 1362 (Opie, 17). Such rhymes make up a good portion of the rhymes parents still share with their children. Margaret Mahler has commented on the importance of games, such as those accompanying these rhymes, for a child's emerging selfhood; indeed, from about seven months of age, infants seem to seek such games, eagerly engaging in peekaboo and pat-a-cake activities. Such games "serve to delineate the infant's own body-image" from the mother's; mother in turn "responds to the baby's emerging playful experimentations with body feelings by playing games of comparing the baby's body parts with her own. . . . To be found by mother, to be seen by her (that is to say, mirrored by her) seems to build body self-awareness, which we must surmise from observation of the endless pleasure in this repetitive game" (Mahler, 221–22).

One of the most common repetitive games involves clapping:

Pat-a-cake, pat-a-cake, baker's man,
Bake me a cake as fast as you can;

Pat it and prick it, and mark it with B,
Put it in the oven for baby and me. (no. 396)

Another clapping rhyme is the famous "Pease porridge hot" (400), as well as this rhyme, cited earlier:

Clap hands, clap hands,
   Till father comes home;
For father's got money,
   But mother's got none. (no. 200)

Clapping the hands together, whether simply observed by the infant in the speaker or whether the speaker takes the infant's hands and claps them, tends to emphasize their separateness as well as the voluntary control of them. It is also the least threatening of these amusements. In contrast, tickling has definite aggressive components:

Round and round the garden
Like a teddy bear;
One step, two step,
Tickle you under there! (no. 177)

The accompanying action to this rhyme traces circles around the child's palm, then the "steps" move up the arm until the child is tickled under the armpit. A more threatening tickling rhyme is:

A good child, a good child,
As I suppose you'll be,
You'll neither laugh nor smile,
At the tickling of your knee. (B-G, no. 583)

Another version ends, "If you laugh, you don't love me." Such rhymes and accompanying actions suggest not only aggression in their impossible demands—they seem both to want and not want the resultant laughter—but sexual stimulation as well; tickling as a prelude to or substitution for sexual contact is practiced by older children. (The Opies cite a comment in 1890 about this rhyme to the effect that it was not meant for children, "the meaning not being exactly decent" [Opie, 184]). Such rhymes stimulate the child and demand its self-control at the same time, making them a minilesson in the problems of living within a culture.

One rhyme offers a combination of tickling and patting, and again suggests a form of sadism:

Is John Smith within?
Yes, that he is.
Can he set a shoe?
Aye, marry, two;
Here a nail and there a nail,
Tick, tack, too. (no. 278)

This rhyme accompanies the patting or tapping of the soles of the baby's feet, miming the driving of nails into a shoe. Since the soles of the feet, especially in children, are highly sensitive, such an activity seems, like tickling, a curious cross between torture and pleasure giving, a borderline sensation, which, like the others represented by these rhymes, human beings seem to seek out.

Several rhymes accompany various forms of bouncing, or knee dandling; they describe "dancing" or "riding" while the child is bounced on the adult's lap, knee, or foot:

Dance a baby, diddy,
What can mammy do wid'e,
    But sit in her lap,
    And give 'un some pap,
And dance a baby diddy? (no. 18)

Ride a cock-horse to Banbury Cross,
To buy little Johnny a galloping horse;
It trots behind and it ambles before,
And Johnny shall ride till he can ride no more. (no. 28)

Here goes my lord,
    A trot, a trot, a trot, a trot . . .
Here goes my lady,
    A canter, a canter, a canter, a canter . . .
Here goes my young master,
    Jockey hitch, jockey hitch, jockey hitch, jockey hitch . . .
Here goes my young miss,
    An amble, an amble, an amble, an amble . . .
The footman lags behind to tipple ale and wine,
And goes a gallop, a gallop, a gallop, to make
    up his time. (no. 310)

Children have generally enjoyed such rhymes and activities; older children and adults indulge in the equivalents of such activities in the form of swinging, seesawing, horseback riding, carnival rides, and, more recently, off-road riding in jeeps and trucks. The enjoyment of the passive bouncing of these later activities may be related to the early enjoyment of the "dancing" and "riding" that accompanied these rhymes—which are a form of sexual stimulation. (*Dancing* and *riding* are common euphemisms for intercourse even today.) As such, they are practiced entirely unconsciously on the part of the adult, who is passing on the pleasure that he or she experienced as a child but whose infantile amnesia has repressed the nature of that pleasure. The passivity of the pleasure reflects its pregenital origin, but since the stimulation acts on both the anal and the genital zones, it offers a forerunner of genital pleasure. Moreover, the number of such rhymes and their conscious and unconscious enjoyment by adults and children suggests that they are not only a reflection of early genital pleasure but a medium through which it is encouraged and passed on, completely innocently, from adult to child, from generation to generation.

Another common form of infant amusement involves dividing the body into parts. The most popular form of this is the "little pig" rhymes, which count the infant's toes:

> This pig got in the barn,
> This ate all the corn,
> This said he wasn't well,
> This said he would go and tell,
> And this said—weke, weke, weke,
> Can't get over the barn door sill. (no. 410)

> Let's go to the wood, says this pig,
> What to do there? says that pig,
> To look for my mother, says this pig,
> What to do with her? says that pig,
> Kiss her to death, says this pig. (no. 411)

> This little pig went to market,
> This little pig stayed at home,
> This little pig had roast beef,
> This little pig had none,
> This little pig cried, Wee-wee-wee-wee-wee,
>   I can't find my way home. (no. 412)

This group of rhymes is remarkably complex in its concerns. It describes greed, devouring, tattling on a sibling, punishment, attack on the mother (by kissing, which mitigates the hostility and thus reflects the ambivalence), hunger, and separation anxiety: one could hardly wish for a better list of infant fears and desires. As noted earlier in this study, the association of pigs with these concerns remains shadowy, but the ambivalence toward the pig in English culture may reflect the English ambivalence toward children. Edmund Leach, quoted earlier, calls attention to the shame attached to the pig resulting from its being kept in similar circumstances as a dog or cat, and yet killed and eaten (Leach, 162). Macfarlane finds that the English attitude toward children is similarly ambivalent; having a child is regarded not as inevitable or even as a particularly good idea. It is a choice that is weighed against other alternatives—land ownership, for instance (Macfarlane, 70). Children are ultimately "non-utilitarian goods—like pets," who give pleasure by "their smallness, their dependence and their ability to learn" (Macfarlane, 54). Children also, by virtue of their smallness, their dependence, and their ignorance, are a burden and a cost, and not a few parents wish, consciously or unconsciously, to be rid of them. The many references to devouring in the rhymes certainly suggest a strongly repressed desire to devour one's children; indeed, a common form of physical play between parent and child is to pretend to "eat you up."[5] Yet to feel hostility and anger toward one's children, much less to express it overtly, when they were a relatively conscious choice, induces guilt and shame. Possibly, ambivalence about children has been displaced onto the pig, and this may account in part for the rhymes that associate pigs with children, especially since the most popular versions stress *little* pigs. Such rhymes simultaneously insult and threaten the child while they give some dignity to the pig, the reverse of institutionalized behavior; thus they provide a kind of middle ground where we can live with our ambivalence toward both.

The counting of the pigs/toes is only one form of the rhymes that separate the parts of the body. The fingers are divided in "Dance, Thumbkin, dance" (B-G, no. 576), as well as in many finger games such as the famous, "Here is the church, and here is the steeple" (Opie, no. 102). There are several rhymes that divide the face:

> Brow bender,
> Eye peeper,
> Nose dreeper,
> Mouth eater,
> Chin chopper . . . (no. 80)

Here sits the Lord Mayor,
Here sit his men,
Here sits the cockadoodle,
Here sits the hen,
Here sit the little chickens,
Here they run in,
Chin chopper, chin chopper, chin chopper, chin. (no. 311)

Such rhymes are accompanied by touching various parts of the face one at a time, usually ending with "chucking" under the infant's chin. The predominance of the word *chop* in them suggests threat and aggression; two of the rhymes refer to "chop-nose day" (no. 338 and 361). Other rhymes, too, suggest attacks on the child's body. "Put your finger in Foxy's hole" (no. 172) invites the child to put its finger into a hole made by the adult's fingers, whereupon the adult's thumbnail nicks the child's finger.

One of the "less restful infant amusements" (Opie, 177) accompanies this rhyme:

My father was a Frenchman,
A Frenchman, a Frenchman,
My father was a Frenchman
And he bought me a fiddle.
  He cut it here,
  He cut it here,
He cut it through the middle. (no. 174)

Here, the child's arm is stretched out, representing the fiddle, and struck gently with the edge of the adult's hand first on the wrist, then on the shoulder; then at the word *middle* the arm is struck sharply at the elbow. It is interesting that this violence is supposedly practiced by the father, but a father who is a "Frenchman"; the rhyme probably represents early chauvinistic indoctrination, as well as deeper oedipal hostility. The Opies' note describing this rhyme says that the *nurse* performs this violence on the child; perhaps their gentility here, as in other matters, prevents their suggesting that a parent might indulge in it. They do point out that older children often practice this activity in school (Opie, 177). One is tempted to speculate further that such rhymes and activities are the forerunners of the controlled violence of, say, the football field. They provide an outlet for the aggressions that, in Kleinian theory, color the infant's earliest encounter with another human being. Practiced by an adult on a child, they may also represent the threat of castration. If other body parts may be subject to removal, the child reasons, then the genitals are threatened as well.

Several rhymes accompany activity that involves falling. The child is tossed up, or bounced off the knee onto the floor, or some other variation. Indeed, tossing and catching a child is one of the most common play activities between adults and children.

> Catch him, crow! carry him, kite!
> Take him away till the apples are ripe;
> When they are ripe and ready to fall,
> Here comes baby, apples and all. (no. 119)

> This is the way the ladies ride,
> Nimble, nimble, nimble, nimble;
> This is the way the gentlemen ride,
> A gallop, a trot, a gallop, a trot . . .
> And when they come to a slippery space—
> They scramble, scramble, scramble—
> Tumble-down, Dick! (B-G no. 566)

The symbolism of falling is highly complex. Mahler speculates that its importance arises from that crucial period in an infant's life when it begins to walk; the frequent falling and bumping into objects "serve as a kind of aggressivization, a firming up and delineation as it were, of his body self-boundaries. These obligatory experiences help him to integrate his body image" (Mahler, 222). The sexual connotation, preserved in the popular phrase "falling in love" as well as other popular images of couples falling down in embraces, cause falling to have both exiting and anxious components, including guilt (Wolfenstein, 130). The adventure of Jack and Jill falling down the hill suggests sexual liaison, which is then punished with injury. Winnicott, as cited earlier, believes falling forever to be one of the chief anxieties in childhood. As the mark of the clown, falling is funny because as spectators, we enjoy our own triumph and mastery of equilibrium. Children's games that involve falling give great pleasure because they allow such mastery. "Ring o'roses" depends on a carefully timed, staged fall by several children together, which they enjoy greatly; it allows them to fall voluntarily as well as to see others fall, simultaneously encouraging, containing, and punishing a guilty wish (Goodwin, 72–73). "London Bridge," one of the oldest and most pervasive amusements in several cultures, suggests, among other things, the fear that falling can never be eliminated no matter what protections we try.[6] But both these games are adopted by children themselves when they provide their own amusements; they allow them to express their mastery of their bodies as well as their fears.

One of the more original nursery games which the Opies cite is called "American jump":

> American jump, American jump,
> One—two—three.
> Under the water, under the sea,
> Catching fishes for my tea,
>   —Dead or alive? (8)

The Opies offer no opinion about why this is *American* jump (though they cite a French version), nor do the Baring-Goulds reprint this one, despite their avowedly American focus and their frequent citing of the Opie text. In the accompanying game, the child jumps on the "one—two—three" and then after a big jump, wraps its legs around the adult's waist (the Opies consistently identify this grown-up as female). The child's head is then lowered toward the floor on the third line; on the fourth, if the child in answer to the question "Dead or alive?" answers "alive," he is pulled up, or if "Dead," allowed to fall to the floor. There are a number of interesting associations here. The rhyme and its activity suggest the child's fantasy of seeing the adult's genitals from below; in rhymes cited earlier, fishes are associated especially with the female genitals, and the child's head-down position would replicate such seeing or the fantasy of it. The position of the child's legs, too, suggests some sexual content to the activity. Finally, the activity of falling is simultaneously threatening, as indicated by the reference to death, but has its own associations to sexual activity and its attendant guilt for children. One might speculate that such a rough-and-tumble game with its sexual overtones was displaced onto the Americans in this rhyme, just as the father's violence was displaced onto the French in the rhyme cited earlier. At any rate, the ambivalence that surrounds falling is well expressed in this rhyme and its accompanying game.

One of the most famous rhymes that concern falling is neither a lullaby nor an amusement, but it nevertheless deserves attention here because of the complexity of its motifs regarding parents and children:

> Humpty Dumpty sat on a wall,
> Humpty Dumpty had a great fall.
>> All the king's horses,
>> And all the king's men,
> Couldn't put Humpty together again. (no. 233)

According to the Opies, this rhyme is so old that its age could be measured in thousands of years. It is a riddle, the answer to which is an egg, but for centuries Humpty has been represented as a person; the rhyme becomes intelligible "if it describes human beings who were personating eggs" (Opie, 215). Versions of it have been found in many languages, all of which have the same motifs of falling and of irreparable destruction.

The association of falling with sexual activity has been cited earlier. This association persists with this rhyme in a girls' game called "Humpty Dumpty," described in 1883: the girls sit down holding their skirts tightly about their feet; at an agreed signal, they all fall backward and then must recover their balance without letting go of their skirts (Opie, 215). The Opies cite Eckenstein's belief that this game is probably older than the rhyme: no doubt. If any further proof were needed of the sophisticated bricolage of folk materials, this game—with its associations of falling, sexual activity, females, eggs, and the prevention of pregnancy—should provide it.

The rhyme has also attracted significant psychoanalytic attention; various forms of reference to it seem to appear fairly frequently in clinical material. In 1953, analyst Thomas A. Petty cited three of his cases, two children and one adult, who made overt references and associations to the rhyme in their analyses. Petty found that in each case, the rhyme helped the analysand deal with the trauma of the birth of a sibling. One child had a Humpty Dumpty balloon, which he balanced on the firescreen, batted with a broom, and finally bit into, puncturing and destroying it. The second child had a Humpty Dumpty doll, which he handled roughly, stuffing it into a mailbox. In both cases, this activity followed the birth of a sibling. The adult, who also had a younger brother, dreamed of throwing an egg-shaped ball down with great force, while sitting on a wall. In each case, the analysand "undid" the birth of the sibling with the

Humpty Dumpty effigy (Petty, 407–10). Petty felt that the egg and the fall symbolized *both* the firstborn child and the second: for the first, the trauma of the sibling's birth represented irreparable damage to the firstborn's relationship to the parents; the broken egg also represented the new child destroyed in fantasy. Thus this rhyme allows the "attenuated repetition of severe psychic trauma and its mastery" (Petty, 412), and became a therapeutic tool of great value.

Australian analyst Isla Lonie has also cited clinical material directly related to this rhyme. One of his patients, an example of borderline pathology, called herself Humpty Dumpty, saying to the analyst, "There is nothing you can do to mend the broken eggshell." She seemed bent on her own destruction, constantly cutting and injuring herself as if to demonstrate her fragility. Her ego, says Lonie, had an "egg-shell quality" from earliest childhood: she was always "on the brink of terror" (Lonie, 377). Lonie compares the potential of such patients to "yolk and albumen," still imprisoned inside the fragile shell. Therapeutic efforts must take into account the preverbal nature of such analysands' difficulties; for this reason Lonie finds the theories of Winnicott more useful than those of Kohut for such patients, since they communicate not by words but by actions, as do preverbal children (Lonie, 380). In this case, as in Petty's case, the nursery rhyme provided a symbolic link between the patient's present difficulties and those associated with more archaic trauma.

In 1986, analyst Renato J. Almansi cited an early case of his, in which the patient's difficulties had a direct relationship to the Humpty Dumpty motif. This patient too had a younger brother, born when the patient was five years old. After some efforts at deciphering a screen memory associated with the birth of his brother, the patient suddenly remembered an episode that took place when he was four and a half, at about the time he would have learned of his mother's pregnancy. The child, having found a basket of eggs in the kitchen, stood on the kitchen table and dropped the eggs, one by one, onto the floor, watching them carefully. The patient remembered this incident as being completely out of character for him, since he was always good and obedient. Almansi believed that this patient had been affected early by primal scene experiences, and that, despite his parents' efforts to conceal from him the secret of birth, he had made the proper connections by the time of the egg incident. The egg breaking also "witnesses to the murderous aggression mobilized by the news of the baby's expected arrival" (Almansi, 40).

Though Almansi's patient did not specifically refer to himself as "Humpty Dumpty" (he was a European Jew who probably did not know the term), Almansi speculates that the rhyme, so ubiquitous in so many cultures and languages, represents symbolically a complex of birth fantasies, which, in these analysands, refers not only to the birth of a sibling but to the birth of the patient as well, to "vague, inchoate, somatic memory traces of the birth process and of other traumatic perinatal experiences" (Almansi, 46). Although he admits he is on highly speculative ground, he cites the work of Phyllis Greenacre and others on cases of severe free-floating anxiety and its possible connection with difficult birth processes.

Interestingly, despite all the research done on neonates and the increasingly sophisticated research today on infants in utero, very little speculation has concerned the process of birth. Greenacre once noted that serious scientific material seemed to focus on the fetus "right up to the time of birth," and then on the problems of the newborn, without "daring to look at" the effect of birth itself, and more particularly at the "ordinary uncomplicated birth." She commented, "Perhaps birth is inevitably too close to death in our feelings; perhaps the struggle of birth is at once too terrifying and too inspiring for us to regard it readily with scientific dispassion. Perhaps men have too much exclusion anxiety and women too much direct anxiety" (1952 [1945], 14–15). The reception of Otto Rank's work on birth trauma in 1924 also suggests considerable discomfort with any emphasis on the physiological and psychological effects of birth, as opposed to the metaphoric ones.

However, Greenacre was able, at times, to gain from adult dreams and symptoms an idea of the special birth experience of the individual and to have her reconstruction "sometimes prove surprisingly correct" (in Almansi, 47). She found that certain head sensations and headaches reactivated in periods of stress could be correlated with the form of birth experience in the individual, noting, "It does seem strange . . . that the head, containing the most precious heritage, the well-developed cerebrum, should not only be the cause of much of the stress of birth but that it is, at the same time, the very part of the infant most endangered during birth" (1952, 5–6). Winnicott too came to believe that certain analysands were able to bring memory traces of the birth experience to their analyses, noting that constrictions of the head and chest and the experience of being unable to breathe were psychosomatic experiences related to the birth experience, as was the less traumatic sense of the whole body as propulsive object. He also commented on the anxiety of being in the "grips of a physical experience . . . [which one] can neither avoid nor understand" (1958 [1949], 181). Though many find such theorizing suspect, this material does help to explain the long popularity of the Humpty Dumpty rhyme, with its emphasis on fragility and anxiety, as well as the many illustrations of Humpty Dumpty as only a large, egg-shaped head, without a body.[7]

Another aspect of the rhyme, which has tended to be obscured over the years but which is grounded in the birth fantasy motif, is its identity as a riddle. In this it is allied with other riddles about eggs:

> As I was walking in a field of wheat,
> I picked up something good to eat;
> Neither fish, flesh, fowl, nor bone,
> I kept it till it ran alone. (no. 243)

> In marble halls as white as milk,
> Lined with a skin as soft as silk,
> Within a fountain crystal-clear,
> A golden apple doth appear.
> No doors there are to this stronghold,
> Yet thieves break in and steal the gold. (no. 199)

It is not surprising that the mystery and fragility of the egg should have engendered such rhymes; on a deeper level, such riddles reflect the enigma of generation and birth itself, as well as the mystery and secrecy with which parents surround it. What is surprising is that these rhymes, especially "Humpty Dumpty," reveal how much quite young children unconsciously understand the connections between sexual activity and birth, and the overwhelming significance of birth in the configuration of the family. Almansi believes the various names for the egg throughout cultures—Humpty-Dumpty, Boule-Boule, Lille-Trille, Hillerin-Lillerin, Trille Trölle, Gigele-Gagele, Hümpelken-Pümpelken, etc.—"point to closely related couples of slightly different little people as would be the case in two children from the same family" (Almansi, 42). Embedded in such linguistic pairings may also be an unconscious reference to the parents, who are double and yet single, in order to produce the "egg." Doublings of parents become single, to produce a single child, and then again a second child, for further doubling. The riddle quoted above, "As I was walking in a field of wheat," acknowledges further mysteries of identity, growth, and separation; this riddle expresses the inevitability of the process as well as its mystery. "In marble halls" expresses the luxury, beauty, and value of the unborn child, which "thieves break in and steal"; like Humpty Dumpty, it expresses the experience of birth and the irreparable "damage" attendant on it. All this suggests that children have solved for themselves the riddle of the egg in ways that parents can never express.[8]

Winnicott used the term "Humpty Dumpty stage" to describe the moment in a child's life when the baby begins to recognize the mother as separate—a precarious moment. "No longer devotedly held," the child must now balance an inner and an outer life; otherwise it is "liable to irreversible disintegration" (1958, 226; 1965, 75). Kate Greenaway offered a remarkable illustration of the thoughtfulness, risk, and resultant sadness of this psychic moment: above only the first two lines of "Humpty Dumpty," she drew a young child sitting on a high wall, dangling its legs, leaning forward, and gazing into space with a forlorn expression (Figure 8). While Greenaway's illustrations to the rhymes often seem unrealistically pretty, she frequently captures the seriousness behind the play in the somber facial expressions on her children. Her illustration for "Humpty Dumpty" is one of her most insightful, as is the rhyme itself—a remarkable compression of human memories and fantasies about isolation, value, birth, falling, destruction, hope, infancy, and survival into a single metaphor of a falling egg, where we can experience their wonder and mystery.

Falling and fragmentation, represented in "This little pig," "American jump," "Brow bender," "My father was a Frenchman," and "Humpty Dumpty," are among a child's deepest fears. Of Winnicott's five "unthinkable anxieties" for the developing ego—going to pieces, falling forever, having no relationship to the body, having no orientation, complete isolation resulting from no means of communication—the first two, going to pieces and falling, could be seen as causes of the other three: a fragmented, falling body can have no stable relationship or communication with itself or with external

Humpty Dumpty sat on a wall,
Humpty Dumpty had a great fall.

Figure 8. Humpty Dumpty. Illustrations by Kate Greenaway from *Mother Goose*. de Grummond Children's Literature Research Collection.

The Complementary Uses of Holding and Playing   97

objects. The question then arises: why have these rhymes, which so vividly arouse and play on these terrors, survived for so long as part of a parent's everyday play with a child? Are they only a form of vengeful sadism, threatening the child's insecure ego with further fragmentation and destruction? The rhymes do demonstrate such a negative side, operating in tandem with a deep ambivalence about the parent's own childhood as well as that of his or her offspring. However, most children nurtured on these rhymes grow up with healthy egos; might the rhymes be part of a therapeutic process that helps children confront and overcome these fears? We have seen in the previous chapters how the rhymes provide a mechanism of control for negative feelings about animals and about the relationship between the sexes, an internal control which then extends itself outward into the culture. The rhymes in this chapter, as they play on fears of falling, separation, fragmentation, and destruction, also have embedded in them a mechanism of control by which these fears are aroused and then comforted: they encourage symbol formation.

In Melanie Klein's description (1930) of her patient "Dick," a child she diagnosed as schizophrenic but who today would be called autistic, the chief feature of his presenting difficulties was an inability to play. He showed neither affect nor interest in the toys in the consulting room. Gradually, however, he began to manipulate some of the toys and then manifested quite destructive impulses, which in turn caused him considerable anxiety. As he became more able to play, Klein noticed an increase in his vocabulary and in his capacity to express sympathy for the objects on which he vented his aggressions. As Klein saw it, Dick's difficulties stemmed from his inability to "bring into phantasy" the sadistic anger he felt toward his mother's body; as he became able to symbolize this sadism, his emotions were released along with this capacity for speech (Klein, 101–106). She concluded that the ability to form symbols is essential to healthy psychic development. Moreover, the symbolization must constantly grow and change, adapting to changes in the child's own growth and environment, gradually evolving into a healthy approximation of reality.

D. W. Winnicott took Klein's ideas of play and shifted the emphasis from the use of play in therapy to a theory of play as cultural experience. He delineated his notion of the transitional object: that phenomenon which the child perceives as the mother or part of the mother while the real mother is gradually disengaging herself from the intense, mirror-relationship to the child. Winnicott then postulated a space between the mother or mother figure and the child, which he called the "potential space" and which he distinguished from the child's inner world and external reality (Winnicott 1971, 41). In this space, the child may use objects from the external world in some way commensurate with its inner life, or else—paraphrasing Klein's ideas about symbol formation—it may project some "fragment of dream potential" into the external setting (Winnicott 1971, 51). Most important for us here is Winnicott's emphasis on trust in the potential space. Trust is essential because of the baby's dependent state; trust relies on and reflects the mother's adapting to the baby's needs. Only with such trust can the play be fully satisfying, and it is satisfying, even when it generates anxiety, because it leads to the containment of experience. To Winnicott, the interplay between separateness and union in this potential space is the origin of the interplay, in cultural products, between originality and the acceptance of tradition (Winnicott 1971, 99). If the baby is given a chance to play in this potential space with a trustworthy mother or mother-figure, the baby "begins to live creatively"—that is, develops symbols and learns to manipulate them. In other words, the baby finds its link with the "cultural inheritance" and learns to make its own contribution to the "cultural pool" (101).

In these infant amusements, the potential space works to reward trust on the one hand and to engender symbols on the other. When an adult enacts "Brow-bender" or "This little pig" with a child, fragmentation anxiety is certainly encouraged, yet the physical motion that most often accompanies the end of such games is a hug, or a pressing together of the separated parts, along with laughter.[9] In the bouncing and riding games such as "This is the way the ladies ride," the ending is marked by physical resolution—catching and holding the baby tightly or hugging the toddler, even after letting it drop to the ground as in "American jump," again with laughter. Such games may threaten, but they reward the child's trust in the adult with restoration to wholeness and a reinforcement of the cohesive self that the child is working to develop.

Allied with the notion of trust is that of risk. When the child accepts the game, it accepts the risk along with it—the risk of falling, of fragmentation, even—at a deeper level—castration. The child is aware of its complete dependency; when the adult first plays the game and repairs the symbolic damage done in it, the child learns to trust and then to risk again as it offers itself for the game once more. Such play is "precarious," in Winnicott's term, for it exists in potential space, that borderline area between the subjective and the external. Games, with their superimposed order, offer a way to control the risk, to "forestall the frightening aspect of playing" (Winnicott 1971, 50).[10] These infant amusements, with their double order of physical game and rhythmic, rhyming language, combine the risk with the control of it. In Huizinga's words, "To dare, to take risks, to bear uncertainty, to endure tension—these are the essence of the play spirit" (Huizinga, 51).

The manipulation of symbols is encouraged by the language accompanying the games—by the rhymes themselves. The forehead is the "Lord Mayor," the toes are pigs, the arm is a fiddle, the baby a falling apple, the head-down position is swimming underwater, bouncing on the adult's knee is riding a horse or dancing. Although many other things are represented symbolically in the rhymes, these games especially encourage symbolic representation of body parts, further encouraging flexibility in the manipulation of symbols as well as body cohesiveness—both essential for the child's psychic health. For without the rhymes, the games would be only a form of bodily excitement, much of it in the erogenous zones. As Winnicott notes, such excitement in itself threatens playing; it is seduction only and makes play impossible (Winnicott 1971, 52). But the words and their organization into symbolic objects, rhythm, and rhyme, turn these games into real play, into self-healing creativity.

Julia Kristeva suggests that a child's development depends first on its experience of its bodily drives, of desire, then of the recognition of illusion in which the infant, in play, passes from fear to peace (Kristeva, 281–86). Unlike Winnicott, Kristeva finds that the gathering and release of tension are essential to this process, and laughter one of its most important components, signaling the release of the tension and the emergence into a sign system. The popularity and long life of these rhymes, with their rhythm, repetition, and climaxes, suggest that part of their function is a kind of orgastic satisfaction. They are enormously pleasurable in themselves, as attractions to a child's polymorphous sexuality and as forerunners of genital pleasure. As Elizabeth Wright wryly puts it, Klein's child, a sensitive soul from the first, beats its own breast, suffering envy, jealousy, greed, and anger. Kristeva's child "chuckles its way into selfhood" (Wright, 99). Such rhymes as these facilitate these complementary processes, allowing both fear and chuckles. Through them, the child learns to be isolated, without being insulated.

Figure 9. Illustration by Kate Greenaway from
A Apple Pie. de Grummond Children's Literature Research Collection.

A diller, a dollar
A ten o'clock scholar,
What makes you come so soon?
You used to come at ten o'clock,
And now you come at noon.

CHAPTER 5 **Ten O'Clock Scholar**
Learning Culture's
Lessons

Deliberately didactic rhymes are easily recognizable; they teach such lessons as the English alphabet or numbering system, or proper behavior in English-speaking society, and their messages often persist well into the conscious life of adulthood. Many adults, I suspect, recite "Thirty days hath September" to themselves when trying to figure the days in that particular month. But culture has other, less visible lessons to teach; these underlie not only ABC and number rhymes but tongue twisters and rhyming riddles, as well as accusatory and name-calling rhymes, which try to shame children into remembering and behaving. Unlike the previously discussed rhymes, this group seems generally intended for older children, perhaps of school age, since their patterns suggest the concerns of the child who, in classical psychoanalytic terms, is emerging from the oedipal crisis and moving toward latency. Such a child's curiosity about sexual matters, having been only partially satisfied, becomes sublimated into the desire for other kinds of knowing, while the regulatory aspect of the social environment, communicated through the parents and other care givers, evolves into the superego as the child become autonomous.

Ego psychology distinguishes between primary and secondary autonomy. Primary autonomy refers to inborn structures of coping, such as fantasy wish fulfillment in the hungry infant, who imagines it is being fed; such structures remain relatively stable throughout life. Secondary autonomy, an acquired structure, only gradually stabilizes; the child slowly learns various means of coping with its physical and psychical environment, such as projection and introjection, which do not regress under stress (Gedo and Goldberg, 74). From this standpoint, maturation means the mastery of defenses, not "detachment from the depths of personality" (16). The close connection between shaming and remembering, in most cultures as well as in the nursery rhymes, encourages such mastery as well as acknowledges those depths.

Some of the rhymes that teach about social behavior are gently reproving. "Three children sliding on the ice" (no. 99) describes the children drowning, commenting that they should have been at home:

> You parents all that children have,
> And you that have got none,
> If you would have them safe abroad,
> Pray keep them safe at home.

This rhyme probably began as a burlesque of pious ballads intended for adults, but it became popular with children (though the poet Robert Southey at age two "could not bear it"—Opie, 119). Two more famous rhymes offer advice from the birds: the cock tells us:

> For early to bed,
> And early to rise,
> Is the way to be healthy
> And wealthy and wise. (no. 106)

And the wise old owl who lived in an oak offered this object lesson:

> The more he saw the less he spoke;
> The less he spoke the more he heard.
> Why can't we all be like that wise old bird? (no. 394)

(The famously taciturn Calvin Coolidge supposedly had these words over his fireplace—Opie, 341). One rhyme, probably originally directed at servants, was eventually "turned on children" (Opie, 136):

Come when you're called,
　Do as you're bid,
Shut the door after you,
　Never be chid. (no. 114)

Several rhymes contrast good behavior with bad, such as "Ding dong bell" (no. 134), "There was a little girl" (no. 186), and this one:

When Jacky's a good boy,
　He shall have cakes and custard;
But when he does nothing but cry,
　He shall have nothing but mustard. (no. 268)

But some rhymes concentrate exclusively on bad behavior, which occasionally results in physical punishment, as with Tom the piper's son, who was beaten for stealing pastry (no. 510), or Polly Flinders whose mother whipped her for dirtying her clothes (no. 421).

Shaming, however, is one of culture's most powerful weapons; it takes several forms in the rhymes. Some rhymes are overtly name calling:

Cross-patch,
　Draw the latch,
Sit by the fire and spin;
　Take a cup,
　And drink it up,
Then call you neighbours in. (no. 118)

Here's Sulky Sue;
What shall we do?
Turn her face to the wall
Till she comes to. (no. 492)

Piss a Bed,
Piss a Bed,
Barley Butt,
Your bum is so heavy
You can't get up. (B-G, no. 19)

Lyer Lyer Lickspit,
Turn about the
Candlestick,
What's good for Lyers?
Brimstone and fire. (B-G, no. 20)

The latter two rhymes have been suppressed in later editions of Mother Goose, but probably still exist in some form in many households. Sarcasm accompanies shaming also:

> A diller, a dollar,
> A ten o'clock scholar,
> What makes you come so soon?
> You used to come at ten o'clock,
> But now you come at noon. (no. 456)

The origin of the introductory words of this rhyme is still shadowy, but "diller" and "dollar" may be forms of "dilatory" and "dullard"; *diller* is a Yorkshire term for a dull and stupid schoolboy (Opie, 379). Such accusatory, name-calling rhymes as these are frequently used by children to each other, but parents and teachers use the technique as well. Indeed, shaming is one of the most potent regulatory mechanisms in any given culture; its form and target may vary, but its effect is generally the same. The shamed ones remember the transgression, desire not to repeat it, and may take pleasure later in shaming others who commit it, partly as an expression of anger toward those who humiliated them. In classic psychoanalytic terms, shaming helps establish the superego. In ego psychology, this process contributes to the establishment of institutionalized behavior, and demonstrates the interaction between private emotions and public regulation.

One small but interesting study suggests that shaming may account for the popularity of several rhymes that might not ordinarily be perceived as shaming in tone. Jean Goodwin compared nursery rhymes popular with toddlers to a random sample of other rhymes and found that seven out of ten popular rhymes contained shaming incidents:

> Jack falls down. Mary and her lamb are laughed at. Simple Simon has no penny. Bo-Peep does not know how to find her sheep. Boy Blue falls asleep and lets cows and the sheep roam, the boy in the lane and the smallest pig cry. Mistakes and errors are the chief sources of shame in these rhymes. (Goodwin, 1978, 71)

It would seem, from such a conclusion, that children perceive a wide range of behavior as shameful, including mistakes and errors. Goodwin also points out the "small vocabulary of shame" attached to sheep in the English language (someone may be "fleeced," or "shorn" of rank; embarrassment causes one to be "sheepish," etc.) and speculates that the presence of sheep in popular rhymes "may represent one symbolic expression of the developmental conflict around shame" (72). She also found that in rhymes from Mexican and Chinese cultures, as well as English and American, the smallest pig is represented as doing something shameful, such as crying or tattling (72). Goodwin's study is unsatisfactory in several ways, among them her lack of a definition of "popular," her incomplete discussion of how the popular rhymes help toddlers in their developmental task of overcoming shame, and the brevity of the sections and the article as a whole (three and a half pages), which suggests much but develops little. She admits, however, this is a "soft" study, and its usefulness may finally be in its suggestions rather than its proof. Noting her popular rhymes and the kinds of shaming incidents in them, in conjunction with the more overtly shaming and name-calling rhymes just quoted, one gains a sense of how frequently the small child perceives its behavior as shameful, and how often it may remember small incidents that seemed shameful but which adults never notice or completely forget. One also recognizes anew that Freud's assessment of the child's superego, as often harsher than any treatment it has received from its parents, cannot be far off the mark.

Other rhymes encourage less painful remembering, but even these sometimes have darker implications. The most famous mnemonic rhyme in the language, popular as early as 1570 (Opie, 381), is unusual in its straightforwardness:

> Thirty days hath September,
> April, June, and November;
> All the rest have thirty-one,
> Excepting February alone,
> And that has twenty-eight days clear
> And twenty-nine in each leap year. (no. 469)

But "Tom married a wife on Sunday" (no. 509), cited earlier in this study, offers a way to remember the days of the week as well as a direct expression of the misogyny that marks many men's attitudes toward marriage. "Solomon Grundy" also encourages remembering

the weekdays, but suggests, without sentiment, the brevity and ca-
priciousness of human life:

> Solomon Grundy,
> Born on a Monday,
> Christened on Tuesday,
> Married on Wednesday,
> Took ill on Thursday,
> Worse on Friday,
> Died on Saturday,
> Buried on Sunday.
> This is the end
> Of Solomon Grundy. (no. 483)

Another very famous rhyme that encourages memorization of the
days of the week, but which may also have darker undertones, is
"Monday's child":

> Monday's child is fair of face,
> Tuesday's child is full of grace,
> Wednesday's child is full of woe,
> Thursday's child has far to go,
> Friday's child is loving and giving,
> Saturday's child works hard for his living,
> And the child that is born on the Sabbath day
> Is bonny and blithe, and good and gay. (no. 353)

The Opies describe how the proper wording of this rhyme became a
national controversy in England in 1948 upon the birth of Prince
Charles on a Sunday. In every known version, however, Sunday's
child is the favored one, a belief that harks back to the Middle Ages
(Opie, 309–10). Part of the appeal of this rhyme may lie in its suggested abrogation of responsibility; its superstition that the child's
character is formed by the accident of the day of its birth, thus
preordained, relieves both parent and child from accountability for
behavior—the same appeal as popular astrology. Moreover, like the
various astrological signs, this rhyme sets up arbitrary categories of
people; it encourages the perception not only of the days of the
week, but of human lives as discrete entities. As so much of Levi-
Strauss's work has shown, the necessity for such perception seems
basic to human thought, and where the correspondences seem greatest, the divisions are the most arbitrary and persistent. For English-
speaking culture, the rhyme and its popularity suggest the necessity

for parents to perceive their children, and for children to perceive themselves, as separate and different from those closest to them.

As noted earlier in this study, the mastery of language represents the mastery of environment, for it encourages the perception of discrete parts in the flow of experience. The child learns this quite early, when adults respond to its moans or babbles with physical care and sometimes with "translations" of its sounds into language. The value of the nursery rhymes as language-learning aids has been generally acknowledged in much literature designed for elementary schoolteachers. Such discussions usually focus on the pleasure young children find in rhythm and rhyme and on the efficacy of the nursery rhymes as introductions to "real" poetry—by which is usually meant poetry written by identifiable poets. Usually the rhymes are labeled "nonsense verse," with no exploration of what that might mean beyond disembedded language sounds.

The rhymes undeniably encourage language learning. They demonstrate not only the basic phonemes of the language and their combinations, but also the use of pronouns and verb forms in rhymes such as "As I walked by myself" (no. 240) and "I would, if I could" (no. 238). Several are effective examples of the importance of punctuation:

> Every lady in this land
> Has twenty nails upon each hand
> Five and twenty on hands and feet
> All this is true without deceit. (no. 291)

But such discussions as those found in most children's literature textbooks are deceptive, for the rhymes are often syntactically complex and not the simple, repetitive productions most often described in such texts. Also, the pleasure in rhyming may have deeper roots. Martha Wolfenstein speculates that it often has to do with the reduction of responsibility: once the first word has been uttered, the second, rhyming one seems obligatory (Wolfenstein, 182). This is allied in turn to magical thinking and to the ritual powers of the spoken word.

It is my theory, of course, that the rhymes gain their peculiar power because they encode into pleasurable language modes the deepest bodily and emotional concerns. Alphabet rhymes, tongue twisters, riddles, and counting rhymes continue to encode these concerns, but within the context of conscious language mastery and the direct expression of the importance of such mastery for acculturation. Their didactic powers, already formidable, are probably increased by the latent messages related to sexuality and aggression.

One of the most famous alphabet rhymes is "A was an apple-pie," still often reprinted with Kate Greenaway's illustrations. Each letter represents some activity associated with the pie: "E eat it, F fought for it, G got it, H had it," etc. The usual title for this rhyme during the eighteenth century was, "The Tragical Death of A, APPLE-PYE Who was Cut in Pieces and Eat by Twenty-Five Gentlemen with whom All Little People Ought to be Very well acquainted" (Opie, 48). This title probably burlesques titles of literary and dramatic tragedies, but psychoanalytically it also suggests not only the necessity of good manners, polite behavior, and knowledge of the alphabet, but the pleasure in devouring that appears in many other rhymes. Even Greenaway momentarily departed from illustrating her usual well-groomed and polite children when she drew the child who "got it" waving a stick and chasing away other children over the broken crockery underfoot (Figure 9). As is the case with so many rhymes, this one allows the child both to express and control a guilty wish, a device which could not fail to aid the mnemonic process. Another famous alphabet, "A was an archer" (no. 2), offers various social stereotypes for contemplation: "L was a lady, who had a white hand, M was a miser, and hoarded up gold; N was a nobleman, gallant and bold." Embedded in its lines are small lessons in behavior: "C was a Cutpurse, and liv'd in disgrace"; "X was expensive and so became poor. Y was a youth who did not love school." Other versions added a line, so that each letter announced a couplet, giving more opportunity for comment: "D was a Drunkard and lov'd a full pot, His face and his belly shew'd him a great sot" (Opie, 50).

One short ABC rhyme also suggests some lessons in behavior as well as a link between marriage and knowledge:

> Great A was alarmed at B's bad behaviour,
> Because C, D, E, F, denied G a favour,
> H had a husband with I, J, K, and L,
> M married Mary and taught her scholars how to spell;
> A, B, C, D, E, F, G, H, I, J, K, L, M, N,
> O, P, Q, R, S, T, U, V, W, X, Y, Z. (no. 5)

The association of marriage and learning to spell might have strong unconscious appeal for the child just repressing its unsatisfied curiosity about sexual matters in favor of the knowledge that adults offer instead—in this case, knowledge of the alphabet. A little-known second verse to "Peter pumpkin eater," which sounds self-consciously didactic, suggests the same association although with curious logic:

Peter, Peter, pumpkin eater,
Had another and didn't love her;
Peter learned to read and spell,
And then he loved her very well. (no. 405)

Another rhyme also suggests this substitution:

Great A, little a,
    Bouncing B,
The cat's in the cupboard
    And she can't see (no. 4)

Just as the cat can't see, so the child can't see what it most longs to see, but it can assuage its ignorance by learning to spell—that is, to control the language that seems to reveal but instead conceals so much.[1]

One rhyme openly identifies the learning of the alphabet with the imposition of culture in the form of the father:

Here's A, B, and C,
    D, E, F, and G,
H, I, J, K, L, M, N, O, P, Q,
    R, S, T, and U,
    W, X, Y, and Z;
And here's the child's Dad,
Who is sagacious and discerning,
And knows this is the Fount of Learning. (no. 3)

In this rhyme, the father's sagacity is directly related to his ability to perceive distinctions and differences among the sounds of the language, and to assign symbols to those distinctions. The child, passing its oedipal crisis, has just perceived some important distinctions as well: between child and mother, between mother and father, between child and father. Such discernments mark the child's emergence into culture and into the necessity for symbolic thought, as represented by language. The identification in this rhyme between that process and the father establishes the child in a patriarchal culture. The Baring-Goulds cite an American version of this rhyme from 1825 which ends:

> And here's good Mama, who knows,
> This is the font whence learning flows. (B-G, 242)

Here the mother as well as the father represents cultural achievement in her mastery of language, but the difference is instructive. The mother is not identified as "sagacious" as well as knowing, and she does not "discern": for her, and perhaps from her, learning "flows." While both parents use language, that associated with mother is inevitably associated with the body and the satisfaction of bodily needs; the language of the father moves further into abstraction and becomes the only way to bridge the separation between child and parent.

That English-speaking culture offers greater rewards to abstract thinking and the manipulation of language comes as no surprise to anyone who has attended its schools. The implications of this valorization of symbolic thinking is the subject of Margaret Donaldson's signal study, *Children's Minds* (1978). She offers psychological studies as well as common-sense observations to prove that while children do indeed attend to the language in which a problem is posed, that attention is different from adults' attention. The formal system of learning in our culture sets great store by "disembedded modes of thought" (Donaldson, 81), and sheer *linguistic form* becomes very important—a highly abstract concept that young children struggle to adopt but which sometimes seems calculated to ensure their failure. Donaldson cites the importance of freeing language from the concrete, of the child's becoming "aware of it as a separate structure," if the child is to succeed in the formal educational process (90). Children who have already been encouraged in this direction come to school with an "enormous initial advantage" (91). Such alphabet rhymes as those cited above have for two or three centuries provided such an advantage, along with other more deeply embedded cultural messages. In 1725, an editor of the rhymes appended to the last-cited rhyme, in which the alphabet is called the "Fount of Learning," a note pointing out that "no Song can be made without the Aid of this," it being the Gamut and Ground Work of them all" (Opie, 50–51). It would seem that educational wisdom has changed little over the centuries; the perception of language as a discrete phenomenon, made up of discrete parts, remains the root of wisdom and educational success.[2]

There is another group of rhymes that encourage such perceptions, in a slightly different way: the tongue twisters. The Opies include eight of these ditties in their collection, and the Baring-Goulds seventeen. They range from the famous "Peter Piper" (no. 406) and "Betty Botter" (no. 41) to less well-known ones such as "There was a man, and his name was Dob" (no. 136) and "Robert Rowley rolled a round roll round" (no. 445), and one that goes on for three verses, ending thus:

> The twain that, in twining, before in the twine
> As twines are intwisted; he now doth untwine;
> Twixt the twain inter-twisting a twine more between,
> He, twirling his twister, makes a twist of the twine. (522)

Such rhymes encourage the perception of language as a discrete entity, a flexible abstraction, on at least three levels. Since they generally repeat one or two sounds over and over, they draw attention to those sounds as mere sound, not associated firmly with any one concept or any one word. Thus the ear learns to discriminate. When the eye sees such rhymes in print, it also engages in discrimination, the symbol's repetition attesting to its flexibility. Whole words begin to lose their associations in such rhymes, and a word like *roll* appears as a disembodied entity, its meaning lost in its appearance. Finally, since the point is to *say* the rhyme distinctly, it draws attention to speech as really made up of discrete sounds instead of the uninterrupted flow we usually think we hear.

Although many such nursery rhymes seem like nonsense, often—perhaps even usually—there are underlying patterns of meaning, some of them not very far beneath the surface, that make the rhyme comprehensible. In "Hey diddle diddle," for instance, the nonsense is a vehicle or a disguise for the sense underneath. The tongue twisters provide a reverse case: though they seem to make some kind of sense on the surface—"Betty Botter bought some butter"—such empirical "sense" is intended only as a vehicle for the sounds, which in themselves, disconnected from familiar concepts, make no sense.

But of course they are not absolute nonsense. In her essay "On Nonsense," Phyllis Greenacre points out that absolute nonsense "is incapable of representing itself" (1971, 596). The surface meaning of these rhymes combined with the repetition of sounds is the achievement of sanity; it indicates a mastery of the conventions of language on all levels. Such rhymes are a triumph of abstraction and therefore a supreme example of culture at work. Greenacre quotes Cammaerts's statement that poetical nonsense such as that written by Edward Lear and Lewis Carroll arises from "the same matrix as nursery rhymes, viz., the 'innocent exuberance of childhood'" (Greenacre 1971, 593). But as we have seen, and as Greenacre finds in Lear and Carroll, this kind of nonsense may not always be so innocent, and the exuberance may spring from darker sources. Certainly there is exuberance in such rhymes, in being able to say them without faltering and in the pleasure that comes with the mastery of language. But this nonsense springs from knowledge and control, and is the mark of maturity rather than childhood.[3]

Greenacre also emphasizes the *sense* aspect of nonsense, as in the bodily senses, and finds that "the intellect and reason emerge developmentally from the hinterland of the bodily senses, and that the separation of the two areas of functioning is never complete" (1971, 595). Certainly these tongue-twisting rhymes engage body and mind together, and represent the defensive aspect of nonsense, making it a force for equilibrium between the body and mind. In *Through the Looking Glass*, Greenacre notes, Alice must work hard to maintain that equilibrium, and even language deserts her:

> Even the words get out of hand and cannot be relied upon. A variety of verbal switches are utilized with punning based on klang associations, alliterations, spoonerisms, malapropisms, portmanteau condensations, neologisms, etc. Humpty Dumpty [in Carroll's book] tries to master words by making them mean whatever he wants them to, but very often, in the struggle, the words themselves seem to go their own way. In other words, even words lose their identity in losing their uniqueness of form and meaning, and seem to run off in various directions. Sometimes the words seem to maintain two opposite meanings (as indeed may be the case even with well-behaved words,) but in the *Looking Glass* especially, opposites seem like nearly identical twins who are bound in an eternal wrangle as in the case of Tweedledum and Tweedledee. (Greenacre 1971, 608)

The tongue-twister rhymes especially, but also other seeming nonsense in the nursery rhymes, cause words to lose their identity and uniqueness, but unlike the language Alice frequently encounters, these words do not "run off in various directions." They remain tightly reined in by their rhythm and rhyme, thus offering the pleasure of *controlled* nonsense. In their function as cultural communications with a didactic purpose, they are what Greenacre calls communicated nonsense, and "communicated nonsense is a defense against destructive forces" (613). Through such rhymes, a child learns not only the discrete parts of the language, but the control with which to hold them, and child itself, together in a coherent whole.

Leo Schneiderman stresses the therapeutic value of nonsense, noting that it opens auditory possibilities, reassures the child that anxieties can be overcome, helps develop a "sense of proportion and a set of implied standards of candor and honesty," and helps release tension and hostility. Most of all, it alerts children to the artificiality of language, and it "prepares the mind to grasp the ironic and paradoxical nature of what adults call 'reality'" (102–107). That children are probably aware of the irony and paradox in reality has been demonstrated by a study in which children aged three to five were read a story in which words such as *hare* and *quay* were used but not defined. When the children were asked what they thought the words might mean, they defined "hair" and "key" but believed those meanings made sense in the context of the story they had been read (Donaldson, 70–71). This discrepancy was interpreted as an example of "functional asymmetry" in language acquisition: children acquire and use language long before they "understand" it, in the abstract sense. Margaret Donaldson suggests that parents and teachers should therefore "beware" of this tendency of children to "acquiesce in the bizarre" (71–72). But the enjoyment of nursery rhymes with their variety of bizarre people and events suggests that adults and children together have been acquiescing in the bizarre for centuries, despite the culture's devaluation of it in the schools.

Both the Opies and the Baring-Goulds include a relatively large number of riddles in their collections: forty-eight riddles appear among the Opies' 550 rhymes, and sixty-nine of the 884 Baring-Gould rhymes are riddles. The rhyming riddle reached the height of its popularity during the Elizabethan age (Opie, 15); many of the most famous riddles among the rhymes date from that time. But both prose and poetic riddles have had cultural significance for many centuries before that, and their fascination continues even today. One of Beatrix Potter's most popular animal characters, Squirrel Nutkin, uses riddles to torment an old owl, and as we have seen, "Humpty Dumpty" is a riddle.

Some riddles are intriguing descriptions of common objects:

> Formed long ago, yet made today,
> Employed while others sleep;
> What few would like to give away,
> Nor any wish to keep. (no. 169)

[Solution: a bed]

> Two brothers are we, great burdens we bear,
>   On which we are bitterly pressed;
> The truth is to say, we are full all the day,
>   And empty when we go to rest. (no. 79)

[Solution: shoes]

> As round as an apple,
> As deep as a cup,
> And all the king's horses
> Cannot pull it up. (no. 10)

[Solution: a well]

Some are considerably more exotic:

> As I looked out my chamber window,
>   I heard something fall;
> I sent my maid to pick it up,
>   But she couldn't pick it all. (no. 239)

[Solution: snuff]

> Highty, tighty, paradighty, clothed all in green,
> The king could not read it, no more could the queen;
> They sent for a wise man out of the East,
> Who said it had horns, but was not a beast. (no. 220)

[Solution: a holly tree]

And at least one seems gratuitously violent:

> When I went up Sandy-Hill,
> I met a sandy-boy;
> I cut his throat, I sucked his blood,
> And left his skin a-hanging-o. (no. 463)

[Solution: an orange]

Roger Caillois has described the "tournament of riddles" inserted into the Scandinavian saga *Hervarar* as an example of the ritual use of riddles; in such "liturgical" riddles, specific information rather than poetic skill solves the riddle. Such riddles are known as *kenningar*, a word whose root means "to know." These riddles thus become "an ordeal in disguise," like a password; their use represents a "profound tendency in ancient Scandinavian civilization" (Caillois, 153–56). Other civilizations share it, however: there are riddles in the Bible, in Brahmanist religion, in Zen philosophy, and of course in Greek mythology, and many of them carry terrible penalties for a wrong answer. It would seem that knowledge, in the seemingly disembedded form of the riddle, is a highly valued commodity among most human cultures.

Probably the most famous riddle in Western culture is that posed by the Sphinx guarding Thebes, which Oedipus answered correctly to become ruler of the city: "What being goes on four legs in the morning, two legs at noon, and three legs at evening?" Oedipus' answer was "Man," who crawls in infancy, walks upright in adulthood, and uses a stick in old age. The significance of this riddle and its answer is manifold. Oedipus's knowledge was the salvation of the city, and gave him great power. Yet it was also his destruction, for his knowledge was also his sexual knowledge of his mother, and the penalty was greater than the reward: blindness, which symbolizes castration, and exile in humiliation, with other deaths and social chaos emanating from his deed as ripples from a stone cast in water. Man's knowledge, this story tells us, carries the seeds of his own destruction, yet he will pursue it fanatically though warned to desist, as Tiresias warned Oedipus.

This story also suggests that what seems to be disembedded knowledge, ritualistic and "liturgical," the form more important than the content, really carries a specific and terrible meaning; the form masks the chaotic reality underneath. Stuart Schneiderman calls attention to this in his description of his analysis with Jacques Lacan. What is surprising, says Schneiderman, is that, impressed by philosophy and the abstractions of language as we are, we tend to assume that Oedipus's answer was the right one. But "it is not the only one and not even the best one"; Schneiderman offers another answer: Oedipus—the name, the individual, not the class *Anthropos* (Schneiderman, 82). The Sphinx was challenging Oedipus to tell who *he* was, to recognize *himself*. Had Oedipus acknowledged his damaged feet as the key to his identity—*Oedipus* means "swollen foot"—there would have been no ensuing tragedy.

Schneiderman is making an analogy here with the process of psychoanalysis, in which the analysand must acknowledge the specifics of his identity—in Lacanian terms, "the formative role of the signifier in the determination of existence." The termination of analysis implies "passing beyond the condition of Oedipus"; it is a break with the past, the closing of the book of one's personal history, and the moving into the future (83). Schneiderman comments that Lacan acted the part of a questioner, "a Zen master, becoming himself a splendid enigma," so that he might be the "grand Other" who obliged his students to offer better and better answers to his riddles in their quest for self-knowledge (81). The point is that all the abstractions of language mask bodily realities, and although the human quest for knowledge may at times appear to lead to further abstractions, it will inevitably lead back to those realities, to what someone has called the unforgettable and the unrememberable (Mahler, 197).

Géza Róheim[4] has also explored the riddle of the Sphinx, but in conjunction with a famous nursery rhyme riddle:

Two legs sat upon three legs
With one leg in his lap;
In comes four legs
And runs away with one leg;
Up jumps two legs,
Catches up three legs,
Throws it after four legs,
And makes him bring back one leg. (no. 302)

The Opies comment that this is one of the most popular riddles, especially with illustrators. Arthur Rackham's interpretation is representative: a man sits on a three-legged stool with a leg of mutton in his lap, his dog runs in and snatches the leg of mutton, whereupon the man jumps up and throws the stool after the animal and makes the dog return the mutton (Figure 10). The Opies conclude by saying that leg riddles are universal and as "old as the Riddle of the Sphinx" (Opie, 268). Róheim noticed the correspondence as early as 1934, when he arrived at a deeper meaning for the rhyme: it describes sexual intercourse. An observer first sees the male on all fours, then the two legs of the female, and finally one leg, which "mysteriously disappears" (quoted in Mintz, 30). The answer to the riddle of the Sphinx may therefore be the primal scene, which the Sphinx herself

Figure 10. Two legs sat upon three legs. Illustration by Arthur Rackham from *Mother Goose: The Old Nursery Rhymes.* The Central Children's Room, Donnell Library Center, The New York Public Library.

symbolizes in her bodily form (in Greek mythology, she combines three creatures: lion, woman, and eagle—two male symbols and one female).

This is indeed the riddle that most puzzles children, and the answer posed by Schneiderman—the individual, the *one*—suggests further the child's puzzlement at how the primal scene can produce the child itself, one individual separate from the parents. This is the knowledge the child most assiduously seeks, and which is the most assiduously denied; it is the knowledge that language promises to reveal but which it only further conceals. It is certainly possible that all other riddles stem from this one, the most unforgettable and the most unrememberable riddle of all. For riddles present odd couplings, incongruous joinings, which only specific knowledge of the elements can solve:

Long legs and short thighs,
Little head and no eyes. (no. 301)

[Solution: a pair of tongs]

A riddle, a riddle,
As I suppose;
A hundred eyes,
And never a nose. (no. 440)

[Solution: a sieve]

There was a thing a full month old
    When Adam was no more;
Before the thing was five weeks old
    Adam was years four score. (no. 499)

[Solution: the moon]

I'm in everyone's way,
But no one I stop;
My four horns every day
In every way play,
    And my head is nailed on at the top. (no. 237)

[Solution: a turnstile]

Such riddles require specific information to solve, not philosophical cleverness or poetic charm; more importantly, they most often use the body as the reference point. The answer is therefore not only external but internal as well. Their message is that one must look to oneself to understand these strange pairings. That the answer may often be disappointing is well captured in verses by Lewis Carroll:

He thought he saw an Elephant,
    That practiced on a fife;
He looked again, and found it was
    A letter from his wife.
"At length, I realize," he said,
    "The bitterness of life."

He thought he saw an Argument
    That proved he was the Pope:
He looked again and found it was
    A bar of Mottled Soap.
"A fact so dread," he faintly said
    "Extinguishes all hope."

(Quoted in Greenacre 1971, 607)

In their oedipal crises, children discover some of the truth, and learn they cannot be "the Pope." Although this discovery is the beginning of independence for the child, the accompanying disappointment and dissatisfaction may linger on unconsciously, even into adulthood. Lewis Carroll seems to have sensed that disappointment, at any rate. And possibly adults enjoy these folk riddles just as much as children because the rhymes assuage that still unsatisfied longing for a certain kind of knowledge.

Theodore Lidz believes the riddle of the Sphinx psychologically represents the effort toward independence from the mother. Examining the myth within the large corpus of myths about Cadmus and his descendants, he has found that all the Cadmus myths represent attempts to deny the child's dependence on the mother and the power of the mother over the child. Cadmus's soldiers spring from the earth, Dionysius from Zeus's thigh, and Oedipus himself, not nurtured by his real mother but by a substitute, has also escaped a mother's domination. The Sphinx then (the term means "strangler") represents the dangerous mother, the phallic female who will devour if she possesses (Lidz, 42). Oedipus's answering the riddle is his triumph over this mother as well. However, as the myth unravels, Oedipus pays a severe penalty for his triumph, spending his last years blind and in exile, cared for by women (44). The riddling nursery rhymes, as they encourage the perception of knowledge as a mark of maturity, may represent a similar triumph over the mother for the child who learns them. As the child comes to possess hitherto hidden knowledge, the phallic mother diminishes in power and fearsomeness. However, as we have seen, the corpus of the rhymes suggests, as does the myth of Oedipus, that her presence persists in spite of the triumph, and that escaping her power is a battle never fully won.

Martha Wolfenstein made an extended study of children's use of riddles, from which she concluded that the joking riddles so loved by children are indeed a reaction to the "chagrin and disappointment" accompanying the child's unsatisfied early curiosity (Wolfenstein [1954] 1978, 95). Finding that the riddle is the favored joke form for children between age six and age eleven, she elicited definitions of riddles from such children and listened carefully while many children told her various riddles and tried to explain why they were funny. By far the favorite kind of joking riddle for these children was the "moron" joke:

Why did the moron tiptoe past the medicine cabinet?
Because he didn't want to wake the sleeping pills.

Why did the moron throw the clock out the window?
Because he wanted to see time fly.

Why did the moron take a bowl and spoon to the movies?
Because he heard they had a new serial.

It is especially interesting that most adults remember these jokes as
"little moron" jokes; in Wolfenstein's study, the children regularly
dropped the "little" and, in fact, pictured the moron as a grown man
(134). He is "the comic fool of folklore whose absurd behavior and
outlandish mistakes embroil him in difficulties and expose him to
punishment. . . . He represents the child in his impulsiveness and
irreverence, as well as in the presumed naiveté which grants immu-
nity of expression" (Wolfenstein, 131–32). It is this character that
the children know they do indeed resemble, and from which they
must distance themselves as far as possible by dropping the "little"
and by picturing the moron as "probably about forty or fifty years
old" (135). And it may be the childlike in the character that adults
recognize and from which they distance themselves when they specify the *little* moron.

Goodwin's study of popular rhymes, cited earlier in this chapter,
offered further proof that mistakes and errors are a source of much
shame for children (Goodwin, 71–72). One of those rhymes cited as
popular was "Simple Simon," which certainly resembles the moron
riddles:

> Simple Simon went a-fishing,
>   For to catch a whale;
> All the water he had got
>   Was in his mother's pail.
>
> Simple Simon went to look
>   If plums grew on a thistle;
> He pricked his finger very much,
>   Which made poor Simon whistle. (no. 476)

Another rhyme that makes fun of ignorance is "Three Jovial
Welshmen." Here the fools are definitely adults, but distanced from
English adults by being Welsh, and allowing laughter because they
are "jovial" themselves. The several stanzas describe their going
hunting and finding various things which they try to identify:

And all the day they hunted
  And nothing they could find,
But a hedgehog in a bramble bush,
  And that they left behind.

The first said it was a hedgehog,
  The second he said, Nay;
The third said it was a pincushion,
  And the pins stuck in wrong way. (no. 525)

Such rhymes help children conquer their perceived shame and ignorance by allowing them to laugh at someone else's ignorance and
absurd activity—absurd activity which they themselves have imag-
ined, or actually engaged in, making themselves subjects of derision
at times.

Wolfenstein points out that almost all the moron riddles involve a
quest for knowledge of some sort; the moron has heard something
he wants to investigate, or he wants to see something. Wolfenstein
speculates that children posit two kinds of knowledge: the kind
obtained by forbidden looking, which involves terrible hazards, and
the purely verbal kind, represented by riddles, which does not involve empirical investigation (99). Children's enjoyment of riddles
allows them the pleasure of knowing without the risks of seeing. In
Freudian terms, it is a neat resolution to the oedipal crisis, trans-
forming the fulfillment of forbidden wishes into absurd jokes—the
opposite, Wolfenstein notes, of "fairy tale wishfulfillment" (123).
When adults pass on such riddles, they initiate the child into a kind
of knowledge and into a further mastery of language, as they encourage the symbolic combination and recombination of disparate
entities.

The difference between counting rhymes and counting-out rhymes
is occasionally blurred, since what begins as a counting rhyme may
be used as a counting-out rhyme. But the general distinction between them is that a counting rhyme is used to teach the numbers
in sequence, as concepts; a counting-out rhyme is used by children
as a formula to determine who is "It" in a game. The latter is usually
briefer than a counting rhyme, heavily rhythmic, and frequently
gibberish. This discussion is limited to those rhymes that fall most
obviously into one category or the other; both categories are relatively small in the Opie and the Baring-Gould collections, compris-

ing only about nine rhymes each in the Opie collection with the proportion much less in Baring-Gould.[5]

The most famous counting rhymes count up to ten, though other verses (which increase the number to twenty) have occasionally been added. Some of them are incremental or cumulative rhymes; that is, they add objects with each other, so that the act of remembering and repeating them becomes progressively more difficult.[6] The most famous incremental rhyme is probably "On the first day of Christmas" (100); another such rhyme offers images equally energetic but more earthy; after counting up to twelve, it counts back again, in part:

> Ten comets in the sky,
> Some low and some high;
> Nine peacocks in the air,
> I wonder how they all came there,
> I don't know and I don't care; . . .
> Six beetles against a wall,
> Close by an old woman's apple-stall;
> Five puppies by our dog Ball,
> Who daily for their breakfast call;
> Four horses stuck in a bog,
> Three monkeys tied to a clog,
> Two pudding ends would choke a dog,
> With a gaping wide-mouthed waddling frog. (no. 176)

Some rhymes are briefer and less challenging, and probably designed for use with younger children:

> One, two, three,
> I love coffee,
> And Billy loves tea,
> How good you be,
> One, two, three,
> I love coffee,
> And Billy loves tea. (no. 386)

> One, two, three, four, five,
> Once I caught a fish alive,
> Six, seven, eight, nine, ten,
> Then I let it go again.
> Why did you let it go?
> Because it bit my finger so.
> Which finger did it bite?
> This little finger on the right. (no. 388)

One counting rhyme, which counts backward from ten, has been one of the most popular and the most controversial rhymes of all. The rhyme known in England as "Ten little nigger boys" (no. 376) was, according to the Opies, undoubtedly an adaptation by Patrick Green around 1869 from the American song composed by Septimus Winner, "Ten little Injuns" (Opie, 328). As such, it evidently translated its inherent racial prejudice from one despised race, the American Indians, to another, supplying in turn a formula for Americans later to express their own prejudice against the Negroes as it came back across the sea in its new form. The variety of labels for the objects of the rhyme in its English form attests to both the interest in it and the underlying sense that these are defamatory labels: "Ten little Negroes," "Ten little Darkies," "Ten Youthful Africans" (Opie, 329), and in America now, more often "Ten Little Indians."

The rhyme itself, in both the American and English versions, describes the demise in turn of each "Injun" or "nigger," some of them quite violent. They break their necks, shoot each other, cut themselves in half, fall overboard, get swallowed by fish or "hugged" by a bear, get drunk, fall down the cellar, or choke themselves. Such a description of the gradual disappearance of a dark-skinned people through their own carelessness or ignorance, coupled with the pleasant rhythm and the gleeful ending, "And then there were none," can hardly be less than wish fulfillment. In many versions the last nigger or Injun gets married, and that is the source of his demise—misogyny similar to that in the mnemonic rhyme for the days of the week, "Tom married a wife on Sunday" (no. 509). The Opies comment that some versions have attempted to add a "happy-ending verse" in which the last little nigger boy and his wife raise a family, "but oral tradition has discarded this as unnecessarily sentimental" (Opie, 328). Sentimental or not, it runs counter to the message of the entire rhyme. Counting, like learning the alphabet, is an exercise in discrimination. The persistence of this rhyme in both England and America despite many attempts to suppress it testifies to the habit of thinking that seeks to discriminate among human beings; this counting exercise finds a convenient bodily and visual focus for it. Its emotional content, unpleasant though it appears on analysis, probably accounts for its popularity, for as with many such rhymes, it expresses wishes and feelings ordinarily suppressed, putting them into formulaic words that can thus appear to be someone else's.

Probably the most famous counting rhyme of all, "One, two, buckle my shoe," is the subject of an unusual and wide-ranging psychoanalytic study by Thomas Mintz (1966). He first looks at the manifest content of the rhyme:

> One, two,
> Buckle my shoe;
> Three, four,
> Close the door;
> Five, six,
> Pick up sticks;
> Seven, eight,
> Lay them straight;
> Nine, ten,
> A big fat hen. (no. 385)

It seems to suggest a developmental perspective, from the very young child who cannot put on its shoes, through interest in exploring the environment ("close the door"), to playing games ("pick up sticks"), to the mastery of the motor activity of the game ("lay them straight"). But the closing line, "A big fat hen," does not seem to fit the pattern. Mintz then proceeds to an ingenious analysis of the latent content, involving the association of shoe with mouth, door with parents' intercourse, sticks with penis, and "lay them straight" with penile function and control. To Mintz, "the progression in the rhyme is obvious: birth, separation from the breast; interest in pregnancy and parental sexual activities; awareness of the penis and its erections; intercourse. This sequence inevitably leads to pregnancy!" And pregnancy is therefore the meaning of "A big fat hen" (Mintz, 32–33). He adds that nine and ten are the months associated with pregnancy. Mintz goes on to identify this rhyme as a counting-out rhyme, thus associating it with the ancient casting of lots, even with the human sacrifice associated with the Druids (42–43). He sees the rhyme's use of numbers as an effort to invoke magic, and its latent message finally as "I want to be potent" (39). He goes on to cite less well-known lines to the rhyme, which number from eleven to twenty and which deal with more adult concerns such as courting and "maids in the kitchen"; these lines end, "My plate's empty," and once again Mintz finds that this is a birth motif (40–41). For him, the rhyme comes full circle, and these less well-known lines offer support for his interpretation of the more popular ones.

Mintz's essay pulls together a number of elements touching on counting rhymes. One is the mystical power associated with counting. From the point of view of this study, such rhymes initiate the child into the mysteries of the adult world, where experience flows uninterrupted but which language divides into discrete elements. The child learns new perceptions and power when it learns to count, just as when it learns to spell. The ancient associations with magic and Druidical sacrifice that fascinate Mintz are an emblem for the counting, which gives the child new control over its environment. Mintz also notes the association of counting with poetry and music, suggesting that "to the primitive, senseless words . . . were powerful words, and some even suggest that the infant's babblings were their prototype" (37). I would suggest rather that the magic of words and their rhythmic associations with numbers have as their prototype the *adult* language that the infant hears and does not understand, but senses the power thereof. The infant learns the power of sound when it needs are met in response to its crying or babbling, but the imposition of order on those sounds, and the power of that order, must come from adult speech.

Mintz's article notes that counting out is a derivation of counting; it exercises the power of counting on one's fellow human beings, moving counting from abstraction to physical reality, its power openly perceived and acknowledged by the group. The Opies too discuss counting-out rhymes at some length in their introduction (12–15), noting that their origins may lie in the early Celtic numerals, retained after the Roman and Saxon invasions by those in lonely and unmolested parts of the country. The most popular counting-out rhyme in both England and America is this:

Eena, meena, mina, mo,
Catch a nigger by his toe;
If he squeals, let him go,
Eena, meena, mina, mo. (149)

The first and last lines of this rhyme closely resemble the old Celtic numerals and their derivations (see especially Opie, 13), and have variations in other languages that are still remarkably similar. The "nigger" reference is considerably younger, however, earlier versions referring to "tinker" or "chicken" (Opie, 156). The Opies add that the "word nigger is common in American folk-lore but is unknown in any English traditional rhyme or proverb" (Opie, 156). Probably the same racial attitudes that produced "Ten little niggers," which seemed to gain ascendance during the midnineteenth century, acted to produce the transformation of this counting-out rhyme on both continents.

A good proportion of the counting-out rhymes are full of nonsense words: "Hokey, pokey, whisky, thum" (no. 227); "Ickle, ockle, blue bockle" (no. 248); "Inter, mintzy, tintzy, tool, Ira, dira, dominu" (no. 251); "Intery, mintery, cutery, corn" (no. 252); "One-ery, two-ery, ickery Ann, Phillisy, phollisy, Nicholas John" (no. 390). These sound like magical words, such as a priest or shaman might use to effect some transformation, and may come partly from the child's memory of the mysterious words of the adults. In daily life with a young child, one may often hear it mimicking such counting words, making up its own sound combinations before it knows the exact formulas, trying out its own fledgling powers of discrimination and combination on both the external world and the symbolic sounds that represent it.

Older children, as they learn to play games among themselves, generally have a large store of counting-out rhymes that are part of their own lore and language, and seldom shared with adults; here nursery rhymes and schoolyard rhymes overlap. The Opies make a conscious effort to limit their counting-out rhymes to those most likely to be recognized by adults as well as children; the Baring-Goulds include some counting-out rhymes that may be more familiar to children. In rhymes that obviously announce "It" for a game, some of the content resembles those rather violent rhymes associated with jumping rope or other activity performed almost exclusively by children:

> Hinx, minx, the old witch winks,
> The fat begins to fry,
> Nobody home but jumping Joan,
> Father, mother, and I.
> Stick, stick, stone dead,
> Blind man can't see,
> Every knave will have a slave,
> You or I must be he. (no. 221)

> One, two, three, four, five, six, seven,
> All good children go to heaven,
>   Penny on the water,

Two pence on the sea,
Three pence on the railway,
Out goes she. (B-G, no. 627)

The Baring-Goulds cite a variation of the latter rhyme which reads, "All good children go to heaven; When they die, Their mothers cry" (Baring-Gould, 249). Another rhyme collected by the Baring-Goulds asks, "Did you ever tell a lie? Yes, I did, and many times. O-U-T, out goes she, Right in the middle of the deep blue sea" (B-G no. 631).

This darker content, and the accompanying gleeful action of forcing someone O-U-T, suggests associations with exile and death. On a less exalted level, it also demonstrates how well children old enough to play their own games have absorbed the chief message of all these didactic rhymes: the importance of perceiving the flow of experience in discrete segments. This is hardly a lesson exclusive to English-speaking cultures; it is probably essential to psychic survival in any culture. The perception of differences, separations, gaps, makes it possible for human beings to control their environment rather than be controlled by it. The imposition of the alphabet on the flow of sound and the imposition of numbers on the chaos of experience are defenses that English-speaking children must adopt if they are to act in their environment without being overwhelmed by it. Like many of the other rhymes included in this study, and like dreams, these rhymes have both a manifest and a latent content, closely joined, equally necessary for meaning, and equally important for the discharge and the control of destructive or aggressive impulses.

As in the fairy tales, the number 3 seems to have considerable significance in rhymes. There are three men in a tub, three wise men of Gotham, three little kittens, an old woman with three sons, another old woman with three cows, etc. Alan Dundes has thoroughly explored the meaning of this number for Americans, and notes that "the child is conditioned by his folklore to expect three and his culture does not disappoint him" (1980, 159).

Bruno Bettelheim explored the number 3 in the fairy tales, pointing out that many tales focus on the third child, who is often identified as the simpleton yet with whom the child hearing the tale identifies. Bettelheim speculates that the number 3 itself, in the child's unconscious, refers to the child, because it perceives itself against the two of its parents no matter what its position among its siblings: "within the most basic family constellation the child is third down" (Bettelheim, 106). A further psychoanalytic significance of three is the visible sex characteristics of each gender: breasts and pubis for females, penis and testes for males. Bettelheim speculates that 3 may therefore refer to the search for one's biological identity, which expands inevitably into the search for personal and social identity (220).

Bettelheim's speculations have validity for both the rhymes and the tales. More importantly here, counting rhymes encourage the child to move beyond the configuration of three—parents and child—into the wider world of four or more. As long as a child can count only to three, it cannot function in the culture; though it is aware of the culture's presence, especially as represented by the position of the father but also as represented by language and numbers and the power they bestow, it cannot manipulate enough elements in it to achieve autonomy. When parents and other adults offer counting and alphabet rhymes to children, they offer to the child the symbols with which to make its own cultural discoveries and contributions; they offer it the means with which to free itself from the configuration of the number 3. Moreover, these symbols are embedded in powerful fantasy, creating brief, rhythmic images and narratives, which speak both to and from the child's body, engaging its earliest, most pleasurable, most disturbing memories.

The legacy of Freud's *Civilization and Its Discontents* has been one of culture as prison, an image that neglects the necessarily pleasurable and enticing aspects of culture. The imposition of order on the unrememberable and the unforgettable represented in the didactic rhymes is rather a gift from culture to individual, from parent to child, bestowed in the spirit of play, no less pleasurable for being essential.

Humpty Dumpty sat on a wall,
Humpty Dumpty had a great fall.
All of the horses, the women and men,
Put Humpty Dumpty together again.
                              —*Father Gander*

CHAPTER 6 **Putting Humpty Dumpty**
Together Again
Rewriting Nursery
Rhymes

Nursery rhymes have always been rewritten, in one form or another. They share this fluidity with the fairy tales, but though the tales' myriad versions have been a continuing subject of scholarly study from Vladimir Propp to Jack Zipes, changes in the rhymes have attracted little systematic analysis. I am not attempting here to cover this complex subject completely, but to offer brief examples of the kinds of revisions that have recurred, along with their possible motives, and to summarize one view of the relationship between culture and the individual, which helps explain the shifting emphases on and dissemination of the rhymes.

The first and most obvious kind of revision noticeable in the rhymes is in some individual words. Sometimes spellings change; "babby" became "baby" in one lullaby. Often words are substituted for other words, such as in one version of "Rub a dub dub" in which "They all jumped out of a *roasted* potato" instead of a "*rotten* potato." Sometimes rhyming words change because pronunciation

Figure 11. Illustration by Randolph Caldecott
for *Sing a Song for Sixpence.* de Grummond
Children's Literature Research Collection.

changes; "Old Mother Hubbard" offers a relic of such changes when it rhymes "coffin" with "laughing." One has only to glance at random through the Opie *Dictionary* and read the notes after each rhyme, to find many examples of such changes and to come to the conclusion that no single wording is "correct." Here, for instance, is a partial listing of the changes the Opies cite in "Hey diddle diddle":

> "the little Dog barked to see the sport and the Maid ran away with the Spoon, Sir" . . . "And the dish lick't up the spoon" . . . "High diddle diddle, The Cat and Fiddle, The Cow leap'd o'er the Moon, The Dog he laugh'd, To see such craft, And the dish ran of[f] with the spoon" . . . the goats jumped over the moon . . . the cat ran away with the spoon." (Opie, 205)

For "Jack Sprat," the Opies cite a version that read, "Jack Sprat he loved no fat, and his wife she lov'ed no lean; And yet betwixt them both, they lick't the platters clean," and another that expanded to "So 'twixt them both they cleared the cloth, and lick'd the platter clean" (238). Since most rhymes have tended until recently to be orally transmitted, such revisions in the rhymes probably result from the inevitable changes in language over the centuries, and in the way people, when repeating something told to them, tend to substitute parallel wording for what they actually heard. As folklorists, the Opies were tireless in collecting as many such variations as they could find, and arranging them as chronologically as is possible with such casually preserved material. As folklorists, they generally did not speculate on the meaning of such changes; they simply recorded them.[1]

Also, as many folklorists have noted, parts of one rhyme may appear in another. Sarah Catherine Martin may have written the first printed version of "Old Mother Hubbard" as we know it, but as we have seen, she borrowed her opening verse directly from a rhyme well-known to her contemporaries, "Old Dame Trot." Another example of this kind of transformation, cited by the Opies, occurs in "London Bridge": an early version included lines from an even older ballad, and read, "London Bridge is broken down, Dance over the Lady Lea; London Bridge is broken down, With a gay lady." The Opies use this clue to trace the rhyme back further than the seventeenth century and to explore its continental parallels (274). These kinds of changes too probably result from oral transmission, and may be more or less meaningful depending on their context.

Another kind of transformation has been discussed by Lina Eckenstein in her 1906 book *Comparative Studies in Nursery Rhymes*. Eckenstein notes that a popular name may be substituted in a rhyme for a common one that has fallen into obscurity, and may thus find its way into print and history, though it offers no clue to the rhyme's origin. She traces the rhyme, "When good King Arthur rul'd the land," through other versions that refer to King Stephen and then to Queen Elizabeth, and offers a poem about King Arthur that bears distinct resemblance to "Old King Cole" (16–19). On the other hand, she points out, famous names such as Jack and Jill can appear in many different rhymes simply because they are very old names—probably from Norse mythology (21). Working within the tradition of comparative folklore, Eckenstein draws mostly parallels instead of conclusions, and some of her speculations have probably been discredited by later scholars. But she does call attention to the rhymes' generic forms, into which many specific references can fit, and the proper names in them, around which many forms may develop.

Their flexibility makes the rhymes perfect vehicles for expressing individual or contemporary concerns. The illustrator Randolph Caldecott made a subtle change in one rhyme, which allowed him to comment on one of the less pleasant ways children learn about money and about adults' seemingly capricious control over it. Instead of "Sing a song *of* sixpence," Caldecott chose to illustrate "Sing a song *for* sixpence": An elderly lady, visiting a family of children, holds up a coin as if in proffered reward for some performance, while the children frown at her (Figure 11). And while Feodor Rojankovsky did not rewrite "Humpty Dumpty," he certainly inserted a contemporary point of view when in his 1942 *Tall Book of Nursery Rhymes*, he drew the egg with a distinctly Hitlerlike hairstyle and mustache (48). Such contemporary interpretations in nursery rhyme illustration would make a rich study in themselves.

Many poets have borrowed the various forms of the rhymes and inserted their own words, relying on the rhymes' familiar rhythms and syntax to make their own words more interesting. Some writers imitate nursery rhymes, mostly because they are a joyful, vigorous field in which they can play with words and images. One children's fortune-telling rhyme has prompted such play on contemporary themes: "Tinker, Tailor, Soldier, Sailor, Rich man, Poor man, Beggarman, Thief," became, in the late 1940s, "Army, Navy, Peerage,

Trade, Doctor, Divinity, Law," or "Soldier brave, Sailor true, Skilled physician, Oxford blue; Learned lawyer [or Gouty nobleman], Squire so hale, Dashing airman, Curate pale." And even A. A. Milne tried his hand in *Now We Are Six*: "What about a Cowboy, Policeman, Jailor, Engine-driver, Or Pirate-Chief?" (Opie, 405) More recently, another writer and illustrator of children's books adopted the nursery rhyme form for his poems; Arnold Lobel, in *Whiskers and Rhymes*, reveals his thorough absorption and enjoyment of the old rhymes, even as he writes new ones:

> There was a man
> Dressed all in cheese.
> Certain was he
> That the sight would please.
> Though his neighbors agreed,
> Those clothes looked well on him,
> They ran far away
> From that certain smell on him. (28)

> Clara, little curlylocks,
> Went out among the trees and rocks.
> She met a lion in his lair,
> Which gave that girl an awful scare.
> Her sudden fear was so intense . . .
> Those curls stood up like a picket fence. (18)

Writers such as Milne and Lobel chose to imitate the old rhymes because the folk rhymes are imaginative and funny, and because they offer a convenient and familiar foundation on which to build new rhymes. Similarly, others may parody the rhymes to make their message seem already familiar; for example, in 1948, the British government borrowed a verse from "Who killed Cock Robin" to make a political statement:

> WHO'LL KILL INFLATION?
> I says John Bull,
>   I speak for the nation—
> We'll work with a will
>   And we'll kill inflation. (Opie, 43)

Private corporations as well as public institutions know that the familiarity of the rhymes helps to make their slogans memorable and thus to sell their products, as for example in the adaptation by the brewers of Guinness Stout of "There was a little man, And he had a little gun":

> There was a little man,
> And he felt a little glum,
> He thought that a Guinness was due, due, due. . .
> For a Guinness is good for you, you, you. (Opie, 43)

As we have seen, other kinds of revisions result from shifting notions of what is appropriate for children. For example, the crude ending of the original "Little Robin Redbreast"—"And poop went his hole"—was changed to a less vivid one; and the implied double meaning of "barm"—yeasty foam on beer but also sexual activity— was muted in a later version of "Trip upon trenchers." Jack Zipes has analyzed this kind of revision in the written fairy tale. He finds that as society's view of the functions of such tales has changed over the centuries, so the tales have changed. A tale such as "Beauty and the Beast," for example, seemed an appropriate didactic medium for aristocratic young women in 1743, but fell into disfavor during the late eighteenth and early nineteenth century, because it seemed to encourage fantasizing rather than rational thought. From 1830 to 1900, however, the fairy tale was reinstituted as a tool of socialization, where it tends to remain today along with a number of "complementary . . . theoretical works with a psychological bent" (Bettelheim's is a recent example) that offer guidelines about the proper use of such tales (16–22). In Zipes's view, such shifts cause the variations in humor, digression, moralizing, and attitudes toward gender that one sees in versions of a popular tale.

The social history of the rhymes may very well parallel that of the tales as Zipes has sketched it, though another book—using historical over psychoanalytic methodology—would be required to explore this idea.[2] I suspect that the rhymes may be more resistant than the tales to such changes. They are briefer, more likely than the tales to be shared quickly in a moment of feeding or casual play; thus they seem a more automatic response on the part of the adult— who needs more leisure and thought to share a tale. As the Opies put it, "the mother or nurse does not employ a jingle because it is a nursery rhyme *per se,* but because in the pleasantness (or desperation) of the moment it is the first thing which comes to her mind" (6). Moreover, the rhymes largely depend on their tight poetic forms for their effects; as we have seen, many more verses may be written to a given rhyme, such as those that followed the popularity of "Old Mother Hubbard" in 1805, but they must still fit into the old form to become a part of the rhyme. This would be true as well for borrowings from other rhymes: those borrowings would have to "fit," rhythmically. The tales have fewer such restraints; the greater elasticity of their prose and their more discursive narrative modes may make them more amenable to incorporating a programmatic message.

Despite these differences, the rhymes have often provided a vehicle for contemporary moral messages, just as have the tales, especially since the midtwentieth century. Zipes notes the recent tendency, especially in the United States, to "sanitize" the old tales— that is, to remove their violence and evident sadism—"so that children do not have nightmares or get weird ideas" (23–24). This same movement constitutes the most self-conscious and visible kind of revision in the rhymes. It gained prominence in England in 1949, when Geoffrey Hall produced *New Nursery Rhymes for Old*, in which he rewrote a number of rhymes to remove their violence. "Ding, dong, bell," was changed to:

> Ding, dong, bell,
> Pussy's at the well.
> Who took her there?
> Little Johnny Hare.
> Who'll bring her in?
> Little Tommy Thin.
What a jolly boy was that
To get some milk for pussy cat,
Who ne'er did any harm,
But played with mice in his father's barn. (Opie, 149)

Hall's efforts were widely reviewed on both sides of the Atlantic, prompting another Englishman, Geoffrey Handley-Taylor, to take up the banner by printing in 1952 a bibliography of nursery rhyme reform, which was largely a collection of reviews of Hall's work. Handley-Taylor's introduction to this bibliography is often cited as evidence of the need for such reform. He commented that in an average collection of two hundred rhymes, half of them were "glorious and ideal for the child." The remaining hundred rhymes, however, contain "extensive villainy": devouring human flesh, choking, body-snatching, lunacy, death by shriveling, cases of whipping and lashing, maiming, self-inflicted injury, abandoned children—his list is long and detailed (and printed in full in Baring-Gould, 20–21). Though Handley-Taylor may have overstated his case somewhat, many parents, editors, writers, and booksellers today agree with his general assessment, and try to create additions to or substitutions for the old rhymes, which will be less offensive to their sensibilities and more in keeping with what they feel are enlightened views on such matters.

One such writer is Dr. Doug Larche, who calls himself "Father Gander." In a collection of revised rhymes, he tries to avoid violence and sexism:

> Little Miss Muffet sat on a tuffet,
> Eating her curds and whey.
> Along came a spider and sat down beside her,
> And she put it in the garden to catch insects.
>
> Peter, Peter, pumpkin eater,
> Had a wife and wished to keep her.
> Treated her with fair respect,
> She stayed with him and hugged his neck!
>
> Humpty Dumpty sat on a wall,
> Humpty Dumpty had a great fall.
> All of the horses, the women and men,
> Put Humpty Dumpty together again.

Larche also comments on current issues: Jack Sprat and his wife should watch their cholesterol; Jack Horner should be careful about sweets; pollution might hurt the twinkly little star; and overpopulation should concern a famous old woman:

> There was an old couple who lived in a shoe,
> They had so many children they didn't know what to do.
> So they gave them some broth and some good whole wheat bread,
> And kissed them all sweetly and sent them to bed.
> There's only one issue I don't understand.
> If they didn't want so many why didn't they plan?

Another book from the same publisher is *Mother Nature Nursery Rhymes*, in which Sandy Stryker, Mindy Bingham, and illustrator Itoko Maeno offer some revised verses on ecological topics:

> Sing a song of sixpence
> Paper full of dyes

Four and twenty fishes
Pay with their lives.

Wouldn't it be better
If our paper goods were plain.
We shouldn't want them colored
If it causes so much pain.

    Round and round the world
    To save the pandas everywhere
    One stop, two stop
    Tickle me under there.

Mother Goose and More, by "Dr. Hickey," offers the original rhyme printed in black ink and his "additions" printed in blue. The old woman in the shoe here does indeed beat her many children, but "early next morning, As children awake, She gave each a breakfast Of sweet milk and cake." And Old Mother Hubbard becomes "Dear Mother Hubbard" as she eventually finds some food in the back of the cupboard.

The introductions to these contemporary revisions of nursery rhymes acknowledge that the new versions may not supplant the old ones, nor is that necessarily their purpose. The authors do believe, however, that "lessons learned in the nursery are lessons learned for life" (Stryker et al.) and that offering these rhymes may have a healthful effect over time.

The efforts of such rewriters seem to spring from their belief that the rhymes are memorable chiefly because of their language patterns, and that embedding other messages in them will embed other values in their hearers. Rhythm and rhyme are certainly part of the charm of the rhymes, and a very potent part indeed. Perry Nodelman has pointed out that in their "obvious patterns of rhyme and rhythm and repetition," they make good use of what communications theorists call "redundancy": "that part of our communications with each other that we already know," and the presence of which is essential for learning new information. This redundancy allows us not only to remember but to enjoy remembering (Nodelman, 192–93).

The question then arises: will such programmatic revisions live for centuries, as have the old rhymes? We have seen that "Old Mother Hubbard" has supplanted "Old Dame Trot" in popularity because the revised version seemed to speak symbolically to memories of early childhood in ways the original did not. Might Father Gander's or Dr. Hickey's revisions survive in the same way? Like the 1805 "Old Mother Hubbard," they are disseminated through written forms first, before oral transmission; on the other hand, also like "Old Mother Hubbard," they depend for their effectiveness on our familiarity with rhymes we have known from earliest childhood, when they were conveyed orally, in unguarded moments of contact with an adult. No simple causes and effects can be established in such a complicated set of relationships among authors, audience, publishers, and archaic cultural symbols.

However, these relationships have been addressed without being oversimplified in a famous 1951 essay by anthropologist Melford Spiro, "Culture and Personality: the Natural History of a False Dichotomy." Spiro distinguishes between cultural heritage and cultural heredity: one's cultural *heritage* is the product of interactions with one's parents plus other enculturated people in the environment; one's cultural *heredity* is the product of interactions with one's parents. In the process of becoming cultural heredity, cultural heritage undergoes some distortions as the child assigns different meanings to it or accepts or rejects portions of it according to the child's learning capacity or individual experience (39). This division, with its mediation through the individual, takes differences into account on a wide scale, and helps explain the great variety of forms a culture can take through the individual in what is yet a relatively consistent system of symbols. Spiro's theory is analogous, in this respect, to ego psychology, which emphasizes the great variety of maneuvers that individuals may adopt as defenses and which become part of their personalities, yet remain within normal range.

As part of the English cultural heritage, shared by all English-speaking people to one degree or another, the nursery rhymes are part of a large fund of cultural elements making up that heritage. They become part of an individual's cultural heredity when parents pass them along to their children. Those parents tend to pass along some of the same ones their parents shared with them, but add to or subtract from this kind of lore as their experiences cause its significance to change. For example, a mother or father may remember Jack and Jill as a pleasant rhyme, responding unconsciously to its suggestion of early sexual play or curiosity. Their child, in turn, who perhaps has to cope with the birth of a sibling early in life, might find "Humpty Dumpty" more fascinating, may consequently remember it longer, and thus may be more likely to pass it along to his or her own child. Some parents might know Doug Larche's version of "Jack be nimble" (which says that if Jack can do it, Jill can too) instead of the folk version, if they enjoyed his book, and consequently their child will probably know it. In this sense, the family is a kind of buffer or porous barrier between the child and the cultural heritage, allowing some but not all elements to penetrate (Spiro, 38). Put another way, the cultural heritage resembles the superego; Spiro believes they are different labels for the same phenomenon (36). Both represent potent influences from the past, which become present in the child's psyche (*present* in the sense of both time and space) and bridge the space between that psyche and the culture.

This dynamic also helps explain the supplanting of some elements of the cultural heritage by others, and the gradual shift in the configuration of that heritage over time. With regard to the rhymes, fewer and fewer are becoming part of individual cultural heredities; of the 550 rhymes in the Opie collection and the more than 800 in the Baring-Goulds', most Americans probably know fewer than twenty-five.[3]

However, the rhymes remain part of the cultural heritage as they shift into written culture. A brief visit to a commercial bookstore and a glance at the children's section will show that the number of nursery rhyme *books* on the market seems to increase each year, while the number of rhymes transmitted orally seems to be shrinking. This situation may be partly the result of the advance in technology, which has vastly increased the entire picture-book supply, and also related to the demands of a middle class and its desire for print. It may also result from the enormous appeal these rhymes seem to have for illustrators; there is scarcely a major illustrator working in the children's picture-book field who has not tried his or her hand at interpreting the rhymes, to say nothing of the many less well-known artists who produce inexpensive versions of rhyme books. At any rate, to shift the terminology a bit, the rhymes may be evolving into elite culture rather than popular or folk culture.

On the other hand, children themselves are constantly revising the rhymes orally, and some of their productions provide not only evidence of a vigorous oral tradition, but pungent commentary on the adaptability of the rhymes to contemporary concerns and on the persistence of violence and sexuality in children's imaginations. Folklorist Simon J. Bronner has collected some examples:

Mary had a little lamb
She tied it to a heater
Every time it turned around
It burned its little peter.

Old Mother Hubbard
Went to the cupboard
To get her poor dog a bone
But when she bent over
Old Rover drove her
And gave her a bone of his own.

Jack and Jill went up the hill
Looking for some fun
Jill forgot to take the Pill
And now they have a son.

Jack and Jill went up the hill
To fetch a pail of water
Jill forgot to take the Pill
And now they have a daughter. (Bronner, 80–81)

It would seem that despite the efforts of Father Gander, Dr. Hickey, and others to co-opt the rhymes for what present-day society regards as more virtuous purposes, children themselves continue to use them in one form or another to vent hostility and express an interest in sex. Iona Opie recently commented on the "gruesome and violent nature of children's group-life . . . the scatalogical rhymes and the tales of horror and death," which shocked some readers when she and Peter Opie published *The Lore and Language of Schoolchildren* in 1959. One reviewer at the time said she was disturbed that "in all these 400 close-packed pages there is hardly a game, prank, or custom that is not based on savagery and violence" (quoted in Marcus, 15–16). Iona Opie's response is that such rhymes are "therapeutic—when recited, and giggled over, by a whole bunch of kids of about the same age. That creates a kind of communal courage" (in Marcus, 16). Children, it seems, will have the rhymes, willy-nilly, with their violence and sexuality intact, and will resort to the subversive means of oral transmission in the schoolyard to keep them.

That books of unrevised rhymes continue to sell well, though, despite the wide variety of other poetry and picture books available, further suggests that many parents are rediscovering part of their cultural heritage. This situation, I would like to believe, testifies to the intrinsic power of the old rhymes. Though the survivors may be a mere handful, their sturdy persistence into our electronic culture acknowledges the presence in them of something beyond individual cultural heredity and even the cultural heritage, something that speaks to the invariant psychological elements in human life: the need to give and receive love; rivalry toward siblings because they seek love from the same objects; resultant hostility and frustration as well as love and mutual aid (Spiro 1987, 23–24). Hartmann, Kris, and Loewenstein also comment on the ubiquity of certain symbols, noting that their persistence is "accountable if we keep in mind how fundamentally similar every human infant's situation in the adult world is; how limited the number of meaningful situations is which the infant invests with affect; how typical and invariant the infant's anxieties are; and finally how uniform some of his basic perceptions and bodily sensations are bound to be" (96–97). If nursery rhymes speak to our psyches, as I believe they do, then they speak not directly to issues of material culture such as overpopulation, pollution, and healthy diet, but symbolically to those early loves, rivalries, hostilities, anxieties, and sensations.

A foreword to L. Frank Baum's *Mother Goose in Prose* announces, "Each tale is a delightful discovery. 'So that is what the rhyme means!' we find ourselves exclaiming. Now we can understand just how the cow managed to jump over the moon . . . [our children will] glow with the discovery of what the rhymes really mean . . . as we smilingly thank Baum for helping us answer the eternal question, 'but why?'" (Perkins in Baum, 7–9). Baum, of course, explains that Little Jack Horner was a good boy because he stayed home to help his mother, and that's why he got a plum pie to eat. The cow jumps over, not the real moon, but only a reflected one. The wondrous wise man who scratched his eyes out and then back in again really only wore spectacles, which got askew when he fell into a bramble bush.

Are these the questions that children really mean when they ask why? Do such answers really get at the mysteries of life that children—and indeed all of us—are curious about? I have tried to show that the power of the rhymes lies not only in their language patterns but in their symbolic address to the larger questions of human life: How can one person come from two others? How are we like and not like the animals? How can our bodies seem so whole, and yet in such separate parts? Why learn to read? Why learn to count? Nursery rhymes have no easy answers, but they offer their own wisdom nonetheless. By not revealing their meaning easily, they encourage us to search for it in unexpected places. More importantly, they make the search a shared pleasure for all of us in English-speaking culture. Peter Opie once said, "Good nonsense is wonderful because it frees the mind. . . . And it seems to me that if you appreciate nonsense, then you're *really* getting wise" (quoted in Cott, 91). The rhymes are that kind of "good nonsense." They let us see that in spite of our vulnerability and mystification in the face of the unanswerable questions of human life, we can still search for answers, and laugh while we do it.

NOTES

CHAPTER 1: *Jumping over the Moon*: Finding the Meaning
　　　　　of Nursery Rhymes

1. The following discussion is based on Ingersoll (1984).
2. One rhyme tersely expresses the dream/joke connection:

> What did I dream? I do not know;
> The fragments fly like chaff.
> Yet strange my mind was tickled so,
> I cannot help but laugh. (B-G No. 188)

3. Klein also introduced a refinement to the notion of projection, which she called projective identification, a process in which the object not only receives the projection but is somehow transformed by it. According to Elizabeth Bott Spillius, this idea is the most widely accepted and discussed of Klein's concepts, and also one of the most controversial and confusing (Spillius, Vol. 1, 81).

CHAPTER 2: *Pussy's in the Well*: Ambivalence toward Animals

1. No. 49 means Rhyme 49 in Opie; Opie, 371 (below) means a page-number reference in the same book. See Preface.
2. The Opies note that hanging dogs was probably not considered unreasonable; they cite several cases. See Opie, 393–94.
3. For an interesting though dated discussion of the ritual hunting of birds and its religious symbolism, as well as the frequent conjoining of the robin and the wren in marriage, see Eckenstein, 171–214.
4. The sociological meaning of cruelty to animals has been well explored in Robert Darnton's *The Great Cat Massacre* (1984). Darnton describes an

incident in French history when a group of ill-treated workers engaged in "metonymic insult": they ravished the master's wife by killing her beloved and overprivileged cat, and then took their revenge on the entire bourgeois system by massacring all the cats they could find. Though this act implies gratuitous cruelty, Darnton insists it is really sophisticated "punning with ceremonies . . . a witch hunt, a festival, a charivari, a mock trial, and a dirty joke" (92–101). English nursery rhymes, in contrast, focus most of their cruelty on underprivileged dogs and horses, rather than overprivileged cats. What meaning this has for these respective cultures I leave to other scholars to decide.

5. Eckenstein points out that many early "dialogue stories" had as their theme the acquisition of pigs, since "pigs were esteemed valuable possessions from a remote period of antiquity" (170). She cites a Russian example in which a man sells his soul to the devil for six pigs; the devil is then later cheated out of the pigs by a clever man (167).

6. One rhyme reflects this preoccupation with size: No. 129 in the Opie collection, "As I was going to Derby," describes a wonderful ram, "fat behind" and "fat before," ten yards high, with an acre of land for every leg it stood on, etc.

7. A different form of identification with animals is belief in reincarnation in animal form. Geoffrey Gorer found, as the "most surprising single piece of information" in his investigation of English character, that of his five thousand informants, 252 of them explicitly expressed belief in such reincarnation. They represented virtually every domination except the Presbyterian. Gorer believed this was "not incongruous with . . . the strange complex of [their] attitudes toward animals" (259).

CHAPTER 3: *Wooing and Wedding*: The Relationship between the Sexes

1. Jung's theory of the archetype, while it opened up ways of exploring dreams and literature of all kinds, has also tended in practice to become linked with gender oppositions; the legacy of the animus/anima distinction has obscured Jung's suggestion that men and women may partake equally of masculine and feminine qualities. Recently, feminist scholars have undertaken a revision of Jungian thought, emphasizing the fluidity of the notion of archetype. For them, an archetype is useful because it is transcendent; it allows us to move out of rigid oppositions and gender distinctions, to form and re-form images according to experience and history and according to various stages of psychological development, images which then may be used in a variety of ways (Lauter and Ruprecht, 13–14). Thus an archetype is not unchanging or eternal; even the archetype of the mother, these scholars point out, has been affected by changes in the experience of human gestation and birth, and could conceivably fade away (15).

2. See also Freud, "Medusa's Head" (1922), in which he compares the female genital to the decapitated head of Medusa. The snakes replace the penis, yet the multiplication of them signifies castration. Such an image isolates the horrifying effects of the female genital from the pleasure-giving ones. Freud comments that the Greeks would inevitably create such an image, being "in the main strongly homosexual" (213).

3. The most self-consciously oedipal rhyme in the Opie collection is not a folk rhyme but a "trifle" composed by Samuel Johnson:

> If a man who turnips cries,
> Cry not when his father dies,
> It is proof that he would rather
> Have a turnip than his father. (no. 319)

4. Bettey offers, as an example of the poverty-stricken widow and the problems she caused the community, the case of Nancy Tucker, a forty-eight-year-old widow who, after much shifting from one place to another, was "forced to end her days among total strangers in the parish poorhouse." Her situation shows the odd mixture of harshness and compassion in the administration of the Poor Law at the time, as well as the ambivalence that pervaded the attitudes of society toward such women (122–23).

5. There is one reference to cuckolds in the Opie collection. A 1780 version of "Mistress Mary" substitutes for "pretty maids all in a row," "Mrs. Mary's cuckolds all in a row." The version was accompanied by an illustration. See Opie, 301 and 318.

CHAPTER 4: *Baby and Me*: The Complementary Uses of Holding and Playing

1. Juliet Mitchell offers a helpful discussion of the meaning of these positions in her introduction to Klein's work (Klein, 28). See also Elizabeth Bott Spillius in her introduction to *Melanie Klein Today*, Vols. 1 and 2 (1988), and the papers collected in these volumes, for an exploration of the theoretical foundations and therapeutic applications of these positions. It should be emphasized that despite Klein's use of terminology from pathological conditions, she is positing *normal* states when she speaks of these positions.

2. Mahler's work on separation and individuation laid the foundation for many subsequent studies on infant psychology. Throughout her 1975 book, *The Psychological Birth of the Human Infant*, she stressed the wide variety of behaviors that can be called normal, as well as the importance of symbol formation and creative play for language development and psychic health. Her theories are undergoing reexamination today in the work of Daniel

Stern, especially his book *The Interpersonal World of the Infant* (New York: Basic Books, 1985).

3. Renato J. Almansi, practicing psychoanalyst and consulting editor of *American Imago*, has long noticed the predominance of anal motifs in lullabies (personal communication, August 19, 1987). Also, Freud's hypothesis about the association between toilet training and rigidity of the adult personality was tested by Gorer in his study of English character. He found "an extremely neat confirmation of the hypothesis": a large number of his respondents believed that toilet training should begin during the first few months of life (Gorer comments that they did not seem to learn from experience); such people were correspondingly more rigid in their attitudes toward sexual behavior than those respondents who believed that toilet training was best delayed until the second year of life (Gorer, 123–24).

4. Freud is here citing a paper by Lou Andreas-Salome in which she speculates that toilet training is a child's first encounter with prohibition and an environment hostile to its impulses. Kleinian theory counters that from the infant's first interaction with another human being, it encounters a hostile environment; it cannot have the breast all the time. (See also Winnicott 1971, 92, on the importance of the infant's biting attacks on the breast for its ego development.)

5. See the Opies' note to "I have been to market" (Opie, 259–60) in which the narrator remembers the relish with which eating a child was mimed.

6. The refrain of "My fair lady" in "London Bridge" suggests some social solution, however, a suggestion borne out by an examination of the variants of the rhyme in which the ending refers to a wedding. See the copious notes on this rhyme in Opie (272–76).

7. One is also reminded of the many popular associations of the egg and the head ("egghead"), and of children's drawings at an early age in which the head and body are usually drawn as a single sphere.

8. Rhymes which refer to being in an oven also carry birth associations:

> Baby and I
> Were baked in a pie,
> The gravy was wonderful hot.
> We had nothing to pay
> To the baker that day,
> And so we crept out of the pot. (no. 15)

See also "Pat-a-cake" (no. 396) in which the cake in the oven bears the baby's initial.

9. Kohut discusses the positive enjoyment of separate body parts in both adults and children, and mentions the value not only of "This little pig" but also of "peekaboo" games, which set up and then relieve the tension of separation (Kohut, 118–19).

10. The frightening aspect of chaotic play has been vividly illustrated by an anonymous artist who designed the frontispiece for an 1816 edition of the rhymes. (See Opie Plate VIII, facing p. 180, for a reproduction.) It illustrates no. 487 in Opie, "The sow came in with the saddle," and depicts animals taking over the kitchen. A cat fiddles while a dog dances; a pig with a threatening aspect rocks the cradle so violently it look as if will overturn, while the baby looks innocently out. The dish and spoon teeter on the edge of the cabinet just above the baby's head, while a menacing sow wearing a saddle glowers at the baby. The rhyme itself, however, offers the means of control; after describing the chaos, it concludes:

> Odd's-bobs! says the gridiron,
>   Can't you agree?
> I'm the head constable,
>   Bring them to me.

CHAPTER 5: *Ten O'Clock Scholar*: Learning Culture's Lessons

1. One rhyme calls attention to such insatiable curiosity:

> We're all dry with drinking on't,
> We're all dry with drinking on't,
> The piper kissed the fiddler's wife,
> And I can't sleep for thinking on't. (no. 524)

2. One wonders if the rote-learning methods and the emphasis on speedy recall in "Sesame Street" alphabet exercises provide as rich a language experience. But since they are the products of a human mind as well, there are surely deeper messages in them. Whether they are the same messages as those in the folk rhymes would be an interesting subject for study.

3. Several rhymes are in the form of "self-evident propositions," a rhetorical mode that seems to have been popular with the English:

> Now what do you think
> Of little Jack Jingle?
> Before he was married
> He used to live single. (no. 263)

> There was a little guinea-pig,
> Who, being little, was not big;
> He always walked upon his feet,
> And never fasted when he eat. (no. 197)

These rhymes suggest an attempt to express the unexpressable, allied with the nonsense rhymes in using controlled language as a defense against bewilderment—something adults may often find appealing.

4. In *The Riddle of the Sphinx* (1934). My information here comes from a note in Mintz (1966).

5. Such counts are of necessity approximate. The difficulty is especially troublesome in the Baring-Gould collection, where the total of 884 rhymes is inflated by the inclusion of many brief proverbial sayings and some games. The Opie collection is more tightly organized but contains a good bit of overlap in its categories as well.

6. Bett's 1924 study of the rhymes emphasizes, as does Eckenstein, the possibly religious roots of such rhymes: "It looks as if all these number chants may have grown out of this—the avoidance of the numeral itself, and the substitution of something else, usually something sacred, so as to escape the unluckiness of counting, in the first place; and then the natural development by which each numeral was replaced by the mention of a sacred thing specially associated with that number" (Bett, 56).

CHAPTER 6: *Putting Humpty Dumpty Together Again*: Rewriting Nursery Rhymes

1. As a traditional folklorist, Peter Opie once criticized American folklorists for what he saw as their intrusion into the material, "saying what is right and what is wrong in folklore. . . . A folklorist should just watch, and not participate" (quoted in Cott, 84).

2. One especially tempting idea from Zipes's essay is the notion of maternality. According to Zipes, German fairy-tale scholar Rüdiger Steinlein believes that in the late eighteenth and early nineteenth century, the tales were perceived as threatening to the patriarchy because they recalled the voice of the mother "as first representative of the Other." Maternality is this quality of association with "pleasure, wishes, and desire" over and above "moral instruction and guidance," a quality that would make the tales subversive and would therefore require revisions in them. This same quality of maternality, as I have tried to show permeates the rhymes; conscious or unconscious reaction to it as threatening to patriarchal authority might account for some of the hostility toward women in the rhymes.

3. The Opies believe that most English nursery rhymes are better known in America, and "in the case of the older ones, often known in versions nearer the original than they are in their home country" (Opie, 42).

WORKS CITED

Almansi, Renato J. "Humpty Dumpty: Some Speculations on the Nursery Rhyme." *American Imago* 43 (1986): 35–49.

Baker, William J. "Historical Meaning in Mother Goose: Nursery Rhymes Illustrative of English Society Before the Industrial Revolution." *Journal of Popular Culture* 9 (1975): 645–52.

Baring-Gould, William and Ceil, eds. *The Annotated Mother Goose*. New York: Bramhall House, 1962.

Baum, L. Frank. *Mother Goose in Prose* (1899). Illustrated by Maxfield Parrish. Foreword, Patricia Barrett Perkins. New York: Bounty Books, 1986.

Bett, Henry. *Nursery Rhymes and Tales: Their Origin and History* (1924). London: Methuen & Co. Ltd., 1978.

Bettelheim, Bruno. *The Uses of Enchantment: The Meaning and Importance of Fairy Tales*. New York: Knopf, 1976.

Bettey, J. H. *Rural Life in Wessex 1500–1900*. Wiltshire, Eng.: Moonraker Press, 1977.

Bock, Philip K. *Rethinking Psychological Anthropology: Continuity and Change in Human Action*. New York: W. H. Freeman & Co., 1988.

Bronner, Simon J. *American Children's Folklore*. Little Rock: August House, 1988.

Caillois, Roger. "Riddles and Images." *Game, Play, and Literature*. Yale French Studies, 148–58. New Haven: Yale University Press, 1968.

Caldecott, Randolph. *A Frog He Would A-Wooing Go*. London: Frederick Warne & Co., n.d.

_____. *Sing a Song For Sixpence*. London: George Routledge & Sons, n.d.

Carpenter, Humphrey, and Mari Prichard. *The Oxford Companion to Children's Literature*. London and New York: Oxford University Press, 1984.

Children's Literature 18. New Haven: Yale University Press, 1990.

Cott, Jonathan. "Finding out Is Better: Profile of Iona and Peter Opie." *The New Yorker* 59 (April 4, 1963): 47–91.

Crane, Walter. *The Baby's Opera*. London: George Routledge & Sons, 1877.

Darnton, Robert. *The Great Cat Massacre*. New York: Basic Books, 1984.

DeSantis, Vincent P. "Nursery Rhymes: A Developmental Perspective," *Psychoanalytic Study of the Child* 41 (1986): 601–26.

Donaldson, Margaret. *Children's Minds*. New York: Norton, 1978.

"Dr. Hickey." *Mother Goose and More*. Oakland, Calif.: Additions Press, 1990.

Dundes, Alan. *Interpreting Folklore*. Bloomington, Ind.: Indiana University Press, 1980.

——. *Parsing Through Customs: Essays by a Freudian Folklorist*. Madison, Wis.: University of Wisconsin Press, 1987.

Durham, Margery. "The Mother Tongue: *Christabel* and the Language of Love." *The (M)Other Tongue*, edited by Shirley Nelson Garner, Claire Kahane, and Madelon Sprengnether, 169–93. Ithaca: Cornell University Press, 1985.

Eckenstein, Lina. *Comparative Studies in Nursery Rhymes*. London: Duckworth & Co., 1906. Reissued by Singing Tree Press, Detroit, 1968.

Ellmann, Mary. *Thinking About Women*. New York: Harcourt, Brace, & World, 1968.

"Father Gander" (Dr. Doug Larche). *Nursery Rhymes: The Equal Rhymes Amendment*. Santa Barbara, Calif.: Advocacy Press, 1985.

Freud, Anna. *The Ego and the Mechanisms of Defense*. New York: International Universities Press, 1966.

Freud, Sigmund. *The Interpretation of Dreams* (1901). New York: Avon, 1965.

——. *Jokes and Their Relation to the Unconscious* (1905). The Standard Edition of the Complete Psychological Works of Sigmund Freud, Vol. VIII. Translated and edited by James Strachey. London: The Hogarth Press, 1961.

——. *Three Essays on the Theory of Sexuality* (1905). New York: Basic Books, 1962.

——. *Totem and Taboo* (1913). Complete Works. Vol. XIII.

——. "A Child Is Being Beaten" (1919). *Sexuality and the Psychology of Love*. Edited by Philip Rieff, 107–32. New York: Macmillan, 1963.

——. *Beyond the Pleasure Principle* (1920). Complete Works. Vol. XVIII.

——. "Medusa's Head" (1922). *Sexuality and the Psychology of Love*. Edited by Philip Rieff, 212–13. New York: Macmillan, 1963.

——. *The Ego and the Id* (1923). New York: Norton, 1962.

——. *Civilization and Its Discontents* (1930). New York: Norton, 1961.

Gedo, John E., and Arnold Goldberg. *Models of the Mind: A Psychoanalytic Theory*. Chicago: University of Chicago Press, 1963.

Geertz, Clifford. *The Interpretation of Cultures*. New York: Basic Books, 1973.

Goodwin, J. "The 'why' of nursery rhymes." *Journal of the American Women's Medical Association* 33 (1978): 66–73.

Gorer, Geoffrey. *Exploring English Character*. London: Cresset, 1955.

Greenacre, Phyllis. "The Predisposition to Anxiety" (1941). *Trauma, Growth, and Personality*, 27–82. New York: International Universities Press, 1952.

———. "The Biological Economy of Birth (1945). *Trauma, Growth, and Personality*, 3–26. New York: International Universities Press, 1952.

———. "On Nonsense" (1964). *Emotional Growth*, 592–615. New York: International Universities Press, 1971.

Greenaway, Kate. *Mother Goose*. London: George Routledge & Sons, 1881.

———. *A Apple Pie*. London: George Routledge & Sons, 1886.

Handley-Taylor, Geoffrey. *A Bibliography of Nursery Rhyme Reform*. Manchester, Eng.: True Aim, 1952.

Hartmann, H., E. Kris, and R. Loewenstein. *Papers on Psychoanalytic Psychology*. Psychological Issues Monograph 14. New York: International Universities Press, 1964.

Horney, Karen. *Essays in Feminine Psychology*. New York: Norton, 1967.

Huizinga, Johan. *Homo Ludens: A Study of the Play Element in Culture*. Boston: Beacon, 1955.

Ingersoll, Sheila Most. "Differences in Context and Outlook Between English Folk Rhymes and Tales," *Folklore* 95 (1964): 38–53.

Juvenile Cabinet of Natural History. London: 1806.

Kardiner, Abram. *The Psychological Frontiers of Society*. New York: Columbia University Press, 1945.

Ker, John Bellenden. *An Essay on the Archaeology of Popular English Phrases and Nursery Rhymes*. London: 1834.

Kiell, Norman. *Varieties of Sexual Experience: Psychosexuality in Literature*. New York: International Universities Press, 1976.

Klein, Melanie. *The Selected Melanie Klein*. Edited by Juliet Mitchell. London: Penguin Books, 1986.

Kohut, Heinz. *The Analysis of the Self*. New York: International Universities Press, 1971.

Kristeva, Julia. *Desire in Language*. New York: Columbia University Press, 1980.

Lacan, Jacques, and the *école freudienne*. *Feminine Sexuality*. Edited by Juliet Mitchell and Jacqueline Rose. New York: Norton, 1985.

Lauter, Estella, and Carol Schreier Rupprecht. *Feminist Archetypal Theory: Interdisciplinary Re-Visions of Jungian Thought*. Knoxville: University of Tennessee Press, 1985.

Leach, Edmund. "Anthropological Aspects of Language: Animal Categories and Verbal Abuse." *Reader in Comparative Religion*, 4th ed. Edited by William A. Lessa and Evon Z. Vogt, 153–66. New York: Harper & Row, 1979.

Levi-Strauss, Claude. *The Savage Mind*. Chicago: University of Chicago Press, 1963.

———. *The Raw and the Cooked*. Chicago: University of Chicago Press, 1969.

Lidz, Theodore. "The Riddle of the Riddle of the Sphinx," *Psychoanalytic Review* 75 (Spring 1988): 35–49.

Little Boy Blue: A Collection of Nursery Rhymes. London: Marcus Ward & Co., Ltd., n.d.

Lonie, Isla. "From Humpty Dumpty to Rapunzel." *Australian and New Zealand Journal of Psychiatry* 19 (1985) 372:381.

Macfarlane, Alan. *Marriage and Love in England: Modes of Reproduction 1300–1840*. Oxford and New York: Basil Blackwell, 1986.

Mahler, Margaret, Fred Pine, and Anni Bergman. *The Psychological Birth of the Human Infant: Symbiosis and Individuation*. New York: Basic Books, 1975.

Marcus, Leonard S. "In Search of 'Childish Things': An Interview with Iona Opie." *The Lion and the Unicorn* 13 (December 1989) 2: 7–27.

Mendelson, Sarah Heller. "Stuart Women's Diaries and Occasional Memoirs." *Women in English Society 1500–1900*. Edited by Mary Prior. London and New York: Methuen, 1985.

Mintz, Thomas. "The Psychology of a Nursery Rhyme." *American Imago* 23 (1966): 22–47.

Morrow, Lance. "Africa." *Time*, February 23, 1987.

Mother Goose: The Old Nursery Rhymes. Illustrated by Arthur Rackham. New York: The Century Company, 1913.

Nodelman, Perry. "The Nursery Rhymes of Mother Goose: A World Without Glasses." *Touchstones*, Vol. 2, 183–201. West Lafayette, Ind.: ChLA Publishers, 1987.

Old Mother Hubbard and Her Wonderful Dog. London: printed at W. S. Fortey's, Bloomsbury, n.d.

The Only True Mother Goose Melodies. (1833). Boston: Lothrop, Lee, & Shepard Co., 1903.

Opie, Iona and Peter, eds. *The Oxford Dictionary of Nursery Rhymes*. Oxford: Oxford University Press (1951), 1984.

Petty, Thomas A. "The Tragedy of Humpty Dumpty." *Psychoanalytic Study of the Child* 9 (1953): 404–412.

Pullen, John. "Capitalism in the Kindergarten: The Economic Implications of Nursery Rhymes." *Quadrant* 144 (1979): 58–59.

Rank, Otto. *The Trauma of Birth* (1924). New York: Robert Brunner, 1952.

Rich, Adrienne. *Of Woman Born: Motherhood as Experience and Institution*. New York: Harper & Row, 1976.

Ritvo, Harriet. *The Animal Estate*. Boston: Harvard University Press, 1987.

Róheim, Géza. *Psychoanalysis and Anthropology*. New York: International Universities Press, 1950.

Rojankovsky, Feodor. *The Tall Book of Mother Goose*. New York: Harper & Row, 1942.

Schneiderman, Leo. "Psychological Aspects of Nonsense Literature for Children." *Nonsense Literature for Children: Aesop to Seuss*. Edited by Celia Catlett Anderson and Marilyn Fain Apseloff, 94–109. Hamden, Conn.: The Shoe String Press, Inc., 1989.

Schneiderman, Stuart. *Jacques Lacan: The Death of an Intellectual Hero*. Cambridge, Mass.: Harvard University Press, 1983.

Serpell, James. *In the Company of Animals*. New York: Basil Blackwell, 1986.

Sewell, Anna. *Black Beauty*. Norwich, Eng.: Jarrold, 1877.

Skura, Meredith Anne. *The Literary Use of the Psychoanalytic Process*. New Haven: Yale University Press, 1981.

Spillius, Elizabeth Bott, ed. *Melanie Klein Today: Developments in Theory and Practice*. 2 Vols. London and New York: Routledge, 1988.

Spiro, Melford E. "Culture and Personality: The Natural History of a False Dichotomy." Psychiatry 14 (1951): 19–46.

_____. *Culture and Human Nature: Theoretical Works of Melford E. Spiro*. Edited by B. Kilbourne and L. Langness. Chicago: University of Chicago Press, 1987.

Stern, Daniel. *The Interpersonal World of the Infant*. New York: Basic Books, 1988.

Stevens, Albert Mason. *The Nursery Rhyme: Remnant of Popular Protest*. Lawrence, Kan.: Coronado Press, 1968.

Stryker, Sandy, and Mindy Bingham. *Mother Nature Nursery Rhymes*. Illustrated by Itoko Maeno. Santa Barbara, Calif.: Advocacy Press, 1990.

Thomas, Katherine Elwes. *The Real Personages of Mother Goose*. Boston: Lothrop, Lee, & Shepard, 1930.

Thomas, Keith. *Man and the Natural World*. New York: Pantheon, 1983.

Todd, Barbara J. "The Remarrying Widow: A Stereotype Reconsidered." *Women in English Society 1500–1900*. Edited by Mary Prior. London and New York: Methuen, 1985.

Tucker, Nicholas. "Lullabies and Child Care: A Historical Perspective." *Opening Texts: Psychoanalysis and the Culture of the Child*. Edited by Joseph H. Smith and William Kerrigan, 17–27. Baltimore: Johns Hopkins University Press, 1985.

Waelder, Robert. *Basic Theory of Psychoanalysis*. New York: Schocken Books, 1971.

Wallace, Edwin R. *Freud and Anthropology: A History and Reappraisal*. New York: International Universities Press, 1983.

Winnicott, D. W. *Through Paediatrics to Psycho-Analysis* (1958). New York: Basic Books, 1978.

—————. *The Maturational Processes and the Facilitating Environment*. Madison, Conn.: International Universities Press, 1965.

—————. *Playing and Reality*. New York: Basic Books, 1971.

Wolfenstein, Martha. *Children's Humor* (1954). Bloomington, Ind.: Indiana University Press, 1978.

Wright, Elizabeth. *Psychoanalytic Criticism: Theory in Practice*. New York: Methuen, 1984.

Zipes, Jack. "The Changing Function of the Fairy Tale." *The Lion and the Unicorn* 12:2 (December 1988), 7–31.

INDEX

"A Apple Pie," 110; illus., 102
"A was an archer," 110
Abbott, John S. C., 83
Aggression, 75, 80–81, 129
Almansi, Renato J., 93–95, 148
Alphabet rhymes, 110–13
Ambivalence, 19–20, 38–40, 83–84
American Imago, 148
"American jump, American jump," 91
Amusements (games), 75–101
Andreas-Salome, Lou, 148
Animal Estate, The, 33–35
Animals in the rhymes, 17–40
Anthropology, 9–11
Archetypes (female), 41, 43–45, 68, 146
"As I looked out my chamber window," 116
"As I was going to Derby," 146
"As I was walking in a field of wheat," 95–96
"As round as an apple," 116
Autonomy, primary and secondary, 104
"Away, bird, away," 21

"Baby and I were baked in a pie," 148
"Baby, baby, naughty baby," 79
Baby's Opera, The, 50, 61; illus., 42, 62

Baker, William J., 14
Baum, L. Frank, 9, 143
Beating in the rhymes, 49, 66–68
Benedict, Ruth, 10
Bestiality, 36–37
Bett, Henry, 150
Bettelheim, Bruno, 129–30
Bettey, J. H., 48, 147
Beuler, Jacob, 35
Beyond the Pleasure Principle, 69
Birds in the rhymes, 21, 22, 25–27
Black Beauty, 36
Bock, Philip K., 10
Bronner, Simon J., 141–42
"Brow bender," 88
"Bye, baby bunting," 78
"Bye, O my baby," 80

"Cackle, cackle, Mother Goose," 29
Caillois, Roger, 116–17
Caldecott, Randolph, 31, 134; illus., 32, 132
"Can you make me a cambric shirt," 58–59
Carpenter, Humphrey, and Mari Prichard, 71
Carroll, Lewis, 17, 114, 120–21
Categorization of men and women in rhymes, 46–56
"Catch him, crow! Carry him, kite!" 90

Cats in the rhymes, 21, 31, 33, 70–71
Children in the rhymes: analogous to servants, 24; punishment of, 24–25; analogous to pigs, 88
Children's literature, defined, 4
Children's Minds, 112, 115
Civilization and its Discontents, 20, 130
"Clap hands, clap hands," 51, 85
Coleridge, Samuel Taylor, 81
"Come when you're called," 24, 105
Comparative Studies in Nursery Rhymes (1906), 92, 134
Contes de ma mere l'oye, 3–4
Coolidge, Calvin, 104
Cott, Jonathan, 144–50
Counting in the rhymes, 123–30
Counting-out rhymes: defined, 123, 128–29
Courtship in the rhymes, 56–161
Cows in the rhymes, 28
Crane, Walter, 50, 61; illus., 42, 62
"Cross-patch," 105
"Culture and Personality: the Natural History of a False Dichotomy," 140–41
"Curly locks, Curly locks," 14, 56, 61
"Cushy cow, bonny, let down thy milk," 28

"Dame Trot and her Comical Cat," 33, 70, 133
"Dance a baby, diddy," 86
Darnton, Robert, 15, 145–46
Darwin, Charles, 63
DeSantis, Vincent, 8, 16
"A diller, a dollar," 103, 106
"Ding dong bell," 17, 21; illus., 18; revised, 137
"Doctor Faustus was a good man," 49
Dogs in the rhymes, 21; representing servants, 23, 31–33, 69–73, 145
Donaldson, Margaret, 112, 115
"Dread of Women, The," 43
"Dr. Hickey," 139–40, 142
Drunkenness, 48

Dundes, Alan, 12–13, 20, 39, 59, 129
Durham, Margery, 81

Eckenstein, Lina, 92, 134, 145, 146, 150
Edgeworth, Maria, 24
"Eena, meena, mina, mo," 127
Ego psychology, 20, 25, 104, 106
Ellmann, Mary, 55, 73, 82
"Elsie Marley," 53–54
Essay on the Archeology of Popular English Phrases and Nursery Rhymes (1834), 14
"Every lady in this land," 109
Exploring English Character (Gorer), 10, 21, 24–25, 56, 58, 146, 148

Fairy tales: distinguished from rhymes, 3–6; "Cinderella," 3; "Puss in Boots," 3; "Bluebeard," 4; "Beauty and the Beast," 4, 136
Falling in the rhymes, 90–98
"Father Gander" (Dr. Doug Larche), 131, 138, 139–40, 141, 142
"Formed long ago, yet made today," 116
Fort-da game, 69–70
Freud and Anthropology, 38–40
Freud, Anna, 74
Freud, Sigmund: on jokes, 6–7; on primary and secondary process, 7–9; on sadism, 20; on primal crime, 37; on anthropology, 38–40; on taboo, 38; on beating, 67–68; on *fort-da* game, 69–70; on anality and sadism, 78–79, 84; on culture, 130; "Medusa's Head," 147; on toilet training, 148
"A frog he would a-wooing go," 4, 31; illus., 32

Games (amusements), 75–101
Gedo, John E., and Arnold Goldberg, 104
Geese in the rhymes, 28–29
Gift-giving in the rhymes, 56–59
"Going up hill whip me not," 36

"A good child, a good child," 85
Goodwin, J., 90, 106–07, 122
Gorer, Geoffrey, 10, 21, 24–25, 56, 58, 146, 148; on swaddling hypothesis, 10
"Great A, little A," 111
"Great A was alarmed at B's bad behavior," 110
Great Cat Massacre, The, 145–46
Greenacre, Phyllis, 94, 113–15, 120
Greenaway, Kate, 96, 110; illus., 97, 102, 110

Hale, Mrs. Sarah Josepha, 33
Hall, Geoffrey, 137
Halliwell, James O., 44, 84
Handley-Taylor, Geoffrey, 137
"Hannah Bantry, in the pantry," 45
Hartmann, H., E. Kris, and R. Loewenstein, 20, 25, 83, 142
"Henry was a worthy king," 6–7
Hens in the rhymes, 28
"Here am I, Little Jumping Joan," 53
"Here goes my lord," 86
"Here's A, B, and C," 111–12
"Here sits the lord mayor," 89
"Here's Sulky Sue," 105
Hervarar, 116–17
"Hins, minx, the old witch winks," 128
Horney, Karen, 43
Horses in the rhymes, 22
Huizinga, Johan, 100
"Humpty Dumpty," 10, 14, 15, 91–98, 116; illus., 97; revised, 131, 138, 140–41
"Hush a bye, baa-lamb," 79
"Hush a bye, baby, on the tree top," 81–82; illus., 82
"Hush thee, my babby" (sic), 80, 131

"I am a pretty wench," 52
"I had a little dog and his name was Blue Bell," 23
"I had a little dog and they called him Buff," 23
"I had a little hen," 28

"I had a little husband," 68
"I love little pussy," 36
"I married a wife by the light of the moon," 64–65
Id, defined, 7
"If all the seas were one sea," 6
"If all the world were paper," 50
"If a man who turnips cries," 147
"If I had a donkey that wouldn't go," 35
"If you find a hairpin," 52
"I'm in everyone's way," 120
Ingersoll, Sheila Most, 4–6, 145
"In marble halls as white as milk," 95
Institution, defined anthropologically, 25
Institutionalized behavior, 25, 106
Institutions, primary and secondary, 11–12
Interpersonal World of the Infant, The, 147–48
"Is John Smith within?" 86
"I've been to market, my lady, my lady," 31

"Jack and Jill," 4, 13, 14, 15, 65–66, 134; illus., 2; revised, 142
"Jack be nimble," revised, 141
"Jack Sprat could eat no fat," 64, 133
"Jemmy Dawson," 64
"Joan, Joan, for your part," 53
Johnson, Samuel, 147
Jokes, 6
Jung, Carl, 146
Juvenile Cabinet of Natural History (1806), 19, 23

Kardiner, Abram, 11–12
Ker, John Bellenden, 14
Klein, Melanie: on projection, 11, 145; on aggression, 46, 89, 74, 75–76, 100–01, 148; on paranoid-schizoid and depressive positions, 76, 147; on symbol formation and play, 98–99

Kohut, Heinz, 148
Kristeva, Julia, 100–01

Lacan, Jacques, 73, 117–18
Ladybird, 28
Language mastery through the
  rhymes, 109–15
Larche, Dr. Doug ("Father Gander"),
  131, 138, 139–40, 141, 142
Lauter, Estella, and Carol Schreier
  Rupprecht, 146
Leach, Edmund, 30, 88
Lear, Edward, 17, 114
"Let's go to the wood, says this pig,"
  87
Levi-Strauss, Claude, 26–27, 28, 46,
  108
Lidz, Theodore, 121
Linton, Ralph, 11
Literalization of metaphor, 13
"Little Bo Peep," 8, 14, 15
"Little Boy Blue," 9
"A little cock-sparrow sat on a green
  tree," 22
"Little maid, pretty maid, whither
  goest thou?" 43
"Little Miss Muffet," revised, 138
"Little Robin Redbreast," 27, 136
Little Women, 83
Lobel, Arnold, 135
"London Bridge," 90–91, 133, 148
Lonie, Isla, 93
"Long legs and short thighs," 120
*Lore and Language of School-
  children, The,* 142
"Lyer Lyer Lickspit," 105
Lullabies in the rhymes, 75–85, 148

Macfarlane, Alan, 50, 54, 56, 58, 60,
  61, 63, 88
Mahler, Margaret, 76–77, 84, 90, 118,
  147–48
"Make a rhyme, make a rhyme," 52
"The man in the moon drinks clar-
  et," 48
Margery Daw, 53
Margery Daw law, 23

*Marriage and Love in England:
  Modes of Reproduction 1300–1840*
  (Macfarlane), 50, 54, 56, 58, 60, 61,
  63, 88
Marriage in the rhymes, 61–74
Martin, Sarah Catherine, 133
"Mary had a little lamb," 33, 36;
  revised, 142
Maternality, 150
Mead, Margaret, 10
"Medusa's Head" (Freud), 147
Melanie Klein Today, 147
Mendelson, Sara Heller, 55
Midsummer Night's Dream, A, 37
Milkmaids in the rhymes, 43–44
Milne, A. A., 135
Mintz, Thomas, 9–10, 118, 126–27,
  150
"Mistress Mary," 8, 9, 147
Mitchell, Juliet, 147
"Monday's child is fair of face," 108
Moron jokes (riddles), 121–23
Morrow, Lance, 39
Mother Goose: American usage for
  rhymes, 3, 41; characters as histor-
  ical figures, 14; possible identity
  of, 28
Mother Goose and More, 139
Mother Goose in Prose, 9, 143
Mother Nature Nursery Rhymes,
  138–39
"My father died a month ago," 50
"My father he died, but I can't tell
  you how," 50
"My father left me three acres of
  land," 50
"My father was a Frenchman," 90–91

New Nursery Rhymes for Old, 137
Nodelman, Perry, 14, 16, 139
Noninstitutionalized behavior, 25
Nonsense, 113–15, 128, 144
"The north wind doth blow," 26, 27
"Now what do you think of little
  Jack Jingle?" 149
Nursery rhymes: British usage, 3;
  distinguished from fairy tales, 4–6;

compared to jokes, 6–7; as secondary institutions, 12; sexual allusions and symbolism in, 13; as expressions of elementary concerns of child, 16, 109–10; revisions of, 131–44

Nursery Rhymes and Tales: Their Origin and History (1924), 150

Oedipus, 117–19, 121
"Oh, madam, I will give you the keys of Canterbury," 57
"Oh where, Oh where has my little dog gone?" 31
"Old King Cole," 9, 47–48, 134
"Old Mother Goose," 29
"Old Mother Hubbard," 6, 32–33, 37, 69–73, 133, 137, 140; illus., 72; revised, 139, 142
"Old woman, old woman, shall we go a-shearing?" 54
Old women in the rhymes, 54–55
"Once I saw a little bird," 26
"One, two, Buckle my shoe," 126–27
"One, two, three," 124
"One, two, three, four, five," 124
"One, two, three, four, five, six, seven," 128–29
Opie, Iona and Peter, 14
Overvaluation (in courtship), 46, 56

"Pat-a-cake, pat-a-cake, baker's man," 75, 84–85, 148
Perkins, Patricia Barrett, 143
Perrault, Charles, 3
"Peter, Peter, pumpkin-eater," 46, 111; revised, 138
Pet-keeping, 34–35
"The pettitoes are little feet," 30
Petty, Thomas A., 92
Phallic women in the rhymes, 41–46, 55, 56, 59–60, 67, 68, 71, 74
Pigs in the rhymes, 29–31, 87–88, 146
"Piss a Bed," 105
Poetry (rhymes as), 9
Potter, Beatrix, 115–16

Prevention of Cruelty to Animals Act, 33
Primary process, 7
Projection, 11–13
Projective systems, 12
Propp, Vladimir, 131
Prostitution in the rhymes, 53–54
Psychoanalysis: the id, 7; primary and secondary process, 7–9; repression, 11; projection, 11–13; primal crime, 37; phobia, 38; aggression, 75, 80–81; Lacanian analysis, 117–18
Psychological Birth of the Human Infant, The, 147–48
Pullen, John, 23
"Punch and Judy," 66, 71

Rackham, Arthur, 118; illus., 119
Rank, Otto, 94
Real Personages of Mother Goose, The, 14, 15
Reincarnation, 146
Repression, 11
Rich, Adrienne, 82–83
"A riddle, a riddle," 120
Riddles in the rhymes, 95–96, 115–23
Riddle of Sphinx, 117–19, 121
Riddle of the Sphinx, The, 150
"Ride a cock horse to Banbury Cross," 15, 86
Ritvo, Harriet, 31, 33–35
"Robin-a-bobbin," 22–23
"Rock-a-bye baby, in the tree top." *See* "Hush a bye baby"
"Rock a bye baby, Thy cradle is green," 78
Roheim, Geza, 10, 118
Rojankovsky, Feodor, 134
"Round and round the garden," 85; revised, 139
"Rowsty dowt," 21
"Rub a dub dub," 8, 48–49

Sadism, 20, 79, 85–86, 98
Schneiderman, Leo, 115

Schneiderman, Stuart, 117–18
"Scissors and string, scissors and string," 63
Secondary process, 8–9
"See, saw, Margery Daw," 23
Serpell, James, 30, 37
Sewell, Anna, 36
Shaming (and remembering), 105–07
"Simple Simon went a-fishing," 122
Sing a Song for Sixpence (Caldecott), 138; illus., 132
"Solomon Grundy," 107–08
Southey, Robert, 104
"The sow came in with the saddle," 149
Sphinx, 117–19, 121
Spillius, Elizabeth Bott, 145, 147
Spiro, Melford, 140–41, 142
Stern, Daniel, 147–48
Stevens, Albert Mason, 14, 16
Stryker, Sandy, Mindy Bingham, and Itoko Maeno, 138–39
Symbol formation, 98

"Taffy was a Welshman," 49
Talmud, 55
"Ten comets in the sky," 124
"Ten little nigger boys," 125, 128
"There was a crooked man," 8
"There was a lady loved a swine," 37, 60–61; illus., 62
"There was a little guinea-pig," 149
"There was a little man and he had a little gun," 21; revised, 136
"There was a little man and he wooed a little maid," 4, 41, 57, 61
"There was a thing a full month old," 120
"There was an old man in a velvet coat," 49
"There was an old woman tossed up in a basket," 45
"There was an old woman who lived in a shoe," 13; revised, 138
"There was an owl lived in an oak," 21

"There were three jovial Welshmen," 122–23
"Thirty days hath September," 103, 107
"This little pig," 29, 87, 148
"This little pig got in the barn," 87
Thomas, Katherine Elwes, 14, 15, 16
Thomas, Keith, 19, 20–21, 34, 37, 40
Three (importance of number), 129–30
"Three children sliding on the ice," 104
Through the Looking Glass, 114
"Tinker, tailor," 134; revised, 134–35
Todd, Barbara J., 55
"Tom married a wife on Sunday," 6, 66, 107
"Tommy Trot, a man of law," 64, 68
Tongue-twisters, 113–15
Totem and Taboo, 37–40
"Trip upon trenchers, and dance upon dishes," 52, 136
Tucker, Nicholas, 80, 84
"Two brothers are we, great burdens we bear," 116
"Two legs sat upon three legs," 118–19; illus., 119

Uses of Enchantment, The, 129–30

Vagina dentata, 45

Waelder, Robert, 36
Wallace, Edwin, 38, 39–40
"We're all dry with drinking on't," 149
"What are little boys made of?" 45
"What did I dream? I do not know," 145
"When I was a little boy I lived by myself," 64
"When I went up Sandy-Hill," 116
"When Jacky's a good boy," 105
"When shall we be married," 60
"Where are you going, my pretty maid?" 43

"Where have you been all the day, my boy Billy?" 59
"Where have you been today, Billy, my son?" 44
Whiskers and Rhymes, 135
"Who killed Cock Robin?" revised, 135
Widows, 54–55
Wild animals, 39
"Will you lend me your mare to ride a mile?" 22

Winnicott, D. W., 77, 90, 93, 94–95, 96, 98–100; on transitional objects and potential space, 98–100, 148
"A wise old owl lived in an oak," 104
Wolfenstein, Martha, 90, 109; on the moron jokes, 121–23
Wonderful Wizard of Oz, The, 9
Wright, Elizabeth, 100–01

Zipes, Jack, 131, 136–37, 150
Zoos, 35